D0018352

Copyright © 2016 Live Dead Publishing. ALL RIGHTS RESERVED.

Published by Live Dead Publishing
1445 N. Boonville Ave, Springfield, Missouri 65802

Cover design, typesetting, and interior design by Prodigy Pixel
(www.prodigypixel.com).

No portion of this book may be reproduced, stored in a retrieval system, or transmitted in any form or by any means—electronic, mechanical, photocopy, recording, or any other—except for brief quotations in printed reviews, without the prior written permission of the publisher.

Unless otherwise specified, Scripture quotations used in this book are from The Holy Bible, New International Version®. NIV®. Copyright © 1973, 1978, 1984 by Biblica Inc., TM. Used by permission of Zondervan Publishing House.

Scripture quotations marked (MSG) are taken from The Message. Copyright © by Eugene H. Peterson 1993, 1994, 1995, 1996, 2000, 2001, 2002. Used by permission of NavPress Publishing Group. All rights reserved.

Scripture quotations marked (NLT) are taken from the Holy Bible, New Living Translation. Copyright © 1996, 2004, 2007 by Tyndale House Foundation. Used by permission of Tyndale House Publishers, Inc., Carol Stream, Illinois 60188. All rights reserved.

Scripture quotations marked (NKJV) are taken from The New King James Version®. Copyright © 1982 by Thomas Nelson, Inc. Used by permission. All rights reserved.

Scripture quotations marked (NASB) are taken from the New American Standar Bible®. Copyright © 1960, 1962, 1963, 1968, 1971, 1972, 1973, 1975, 1977, 1995 by The Lockman Foundation. Used by permission.

Pencil drawings provided by Live Dead: Austin Evans, Gabe Tenneson, and Josh Tenneson. Photography courtesy of Live Dead Arab World and Dreamstime.com.

ISBN 978-0-9981789-0-5
Printed in the United States of America

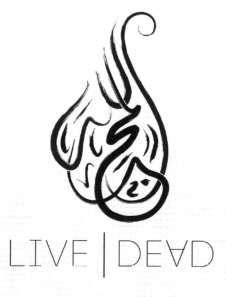

LIVE | DEAD

ARAB WORLD

CONTENTS

Jesus is not yet exalted among the Bedouins of Egypt or the Berbers of Algeria. Islamic fundamentalists and fighters for the Islamic State don't yet confess Jesus as Lord nor bow their knees in reverence. Mothers in Yemen, teenage boys in Libya, fathers in Syria, and female university students in Iraq do not yet lift their voices in praise to the only One who can save them from their sins.

Small pockets of people proclaim His name in some cities of the Arab world. Fewer than five indigenous voices proclaim Him in entire countries. In some countries of the Arabian Peninsula, there are more Starbucks than local believers.

We live in a strange and wonderful day where, since the second century, the Arab world has never been less Christian, and yet never have we seen so many Arab Muslims coming to Jesus. Thirteen percent of the Arab world was Christian in 1900. Today less than four percent of the Arab world is Christian—nominal or otherwise. Persecution, immigration, and high Muslim birthrates all contribute to the decline of Christianity in the Middle East.[1]

As we journey on towards that great and wonderful day when Jesus comes to restore all things, we realize that never before have things been so desperate in the Arab world, and never before has there been so much promise of an outpouring of the Spirit of God.

This book asks you to journey with us as we seek to prepare our hearts for what God wants to do in us and in the Arab world. In God's sovereignty, Arabs are now flooding the nations of the world, so this journey is relevant to us all.

THE DAILY JOURNEY

The journey with Jesus is a daily journey of obedience. It is what author and scholar Eugene Peterson calls a "long obedience in the same direction." The journey's destination is not salvation or heaven or eternity. The destination is to know Him, that He would be our all in all. We are all on a daily journey to know Him.

In these pages you will join the journey of workers in the Arab world—our journey to see the manifestation of God's glory among His workers, among new believers and not-yet-believers, among the rich and the poor, among those bound in false religion. Here we give you a look at Christ being formed in us, workers in the Arab world, as we walk in daily obedience to Him. This walk is not unique to those who work among Arabs; it's just the lens we use to examine the values that are needed to underpin the work of making Jesus famous among all peoples everywhere.

Our journey is not one of grand adventure through the sands of Saudi Arabia and over the mountains of Sinai. It is the hard journey of a porter carrying the King to the lands, peoples, and neighbors yet to be ruled.

THE JOURNEY AHEAD

This is a journey of discipleship for you, through the eyes of a worker in the Arab world. Perhaps God is sending you to this part of the world, to plant the church among the unreached on one of our teams, or maybe He is preparing to do similar work in another part of the world. Let this book serve as your primer. Maybe you're a friend and partner back home, not living with us on the field. Take the principles here and apply to them to your context—because we're all on the same journey of knowing Jesus and serving to see Him exalted among every people group in every city in every nation.

This is a journey through the Arab world, starting in Morocco, crossing North Africa, circling through the Middle East, wrapping around the Arabian Peninsula, and landing in Saudi Arabia. At each of the twelve stops, you will take a walk with a worker through the city, get a glimpse into personal abiding time, and hear stories about how we live out the values of Live Dead.

There are no questions at the end of chapters. You'll find no prompts for discussion. Take as much time as you need in each city. Stay in Tangier for day; stay in Baghdad for a week. Write notes in the margins, or pull out a journal and record your thoughts for later. This is your journey with Jesus.

STOP ONE

A Walk Through Tangier

Welcome to Tangier, the port city on the Strait of Gibraltar. A link to Europe, the city is a strategic gateway for many North and Sub-Saharan Africans seeking a better life in Europe. The oldest city in Morocco, Tangier was originally a trading post for the Phoenicians around 1600 B.C. More recently, from 1922 to 1956, it was an International City, ruled by representatives of eight European countries. The international feel of the city remains today and among its residents are Arab Moroccans, the country's largest unreached people group.

A WALK THROUGH TANGIER

Today is a particularly clear day, and I can see Spain across the Strait of Gibraltar as I walk along the corniche. The continent of Europe is somewhere around eight miles away from us, depending on where one measures.

Until recently, I lived in Cairo, and Tangier and Cairo are vastly different. Tangier *is* a melting pot; it's where Europe meets the Arab world meets Africa. It's easily the most international city I've ever lived in. Spanish, French, and Arabic are widely spoken, and English only to a smaller degree. The Arabic I learned in Cairo is helpful, but I'm still working on the dialect Moroccans speak here.

There are some days I have no idea what to make of this place. In the past it was known as a city of espionage. Remember that scene in *The Bourne Ultimatum*, where Nicky throws her phone on the ground as an assassin chases her? That was filmed here. Not only that, it was filmed at a café famous for its spy clientele. During World War II, no country owned Tangier. Spain, Portugal, France, they all claimed it, but it was neutral ground. Allies and Nazis would sit in the same coffee shops and exchange information. It all sounds like a Hollywood movie, but it's what happened.

I can't help but wonder if a history of not belonging to anyone and a past full of sharing state secrets has left Tangier without an identity. Because the Tangier I walk through today feels like a city looking for itself. My new home desperately wants to be European. It flings its arms wide open to tourists and foreigners alike. Foreign businesses get all kinds of tax breaks here. But its ties to Islam seem to hold its Western dream in check. Life here has a strange and tenuous balance to it.

Tangier almost feels like a tourist town with Europeans coming for day visits, making the city feel like it's always on the verge of a party. On my walks, I often see horse and camel rides and kids playing with remote control cars. And Saturday, it seems, is the day designated for exercise, with men and women out running in the park. Muslim women wear ball caps over their hijabs when they run, which I find curious and somewhat amusing.

Like so many cities around the world, cafes and coffee shops are found on every street here—and there are some great ones that overlook the Atlantic Ocean. The people line their tables and chairs up facing the street, sit with their Moroccan mint tea and watch the world go by. Actually, I've noticed there is a lot of sitting *everywhere*. That's a difference from Cairo. The people of Tangier love the outdoors. I see men on park benches and women sitting with families on the grass watching their kids play. And these people love the beach; the beaches are always full of people. Thankfully, the city and its surrounding Moroccan countryside are very lush and green, perfect for spending time outside.

It's easy for me to find young ladies to talk to. Everything is so close that everyone walks everywhere, and with all the cafes, it's easy to meet people along the way. When I get my directions mixed up, I don't worry because people are very friendly (and I'm from the South so I know friendly). Moroccans will help you with anything—even if they don't speak English, they will do whatever it takes to help. They don't smile all that often but they are extremely helpful—that took some getting used to.

One of my friends with a beautiful smile though is Salma. I met her at a print shop. I needed a visa picture so I could join a local gym; she needed a picture of her daughter to enroll her in daycare so she could get a job. I introduced myself in Arabic—Salma answered in English. As we talked, I discovered she was married to an Indian man who was living in India. She lived here with her mom and child. As our conversation at the shop came to an end, I told her I would love to visit with her again and asked for her phone number. She quickly agreed. "I don't have many friends," she said several times.

"Discipline leads to desire, which matures into delight."

— DICK BROGDEN

Two days later, I met Salma outside a local mosque and we walked down to a café overlooking the sea. There are not many Christian believers here in Tangier, but I find openness to conversations of faith with anyone who speaks English. They jump right into it, if they're open. My conversation with Salma turned quickly in that direction. She told me she had explored Hinduism and Judaism a few years back, and I asked if she knew any Christians. "Yes, I had some Christian friends from Lebanon," she replied. Herself a Muslim, she then recounted a pretty accurate look at what Christians believe. We spent more time talking about Christianity and eventually her views on Islam. Her conclusion: "I don't know. I think I'm right but I don't know. I'm not sure." I pray for my friend. Her search continues—a search for a friend and a purpose. I pray I can be an answer to both.

Morocco is ninety-nine percent Muslim. There are church buildings around the city, remnants, mostly empty. The French and Spanish expats have Catholic and Protestant churches, and I attend an English-speaking international church, but there are no churches for Moroccans. The few Moroccan Muslim background believers in Tangier meet in houses hidden from the eye of the government. I heard that nearly all of those local believers became believers not through foreigners but through locals. Praise God! I thank God for bringing me to a city in search of its identity, and I pray that I will be faithful to proclaim His truth to the people I meet. I believe that Tangier and its people will find their true identity. I believe their search will end, and they will find their place in God's family as His sons and daughters.

EXTRAVAGANT DAILY TIME WITH JESUS
CARRIE EVANS

Abiding is the first thing I do each morning. I love the land and the people I live among, but it's a nation where ninety-nine percent of the people do not know Jesus. The spiritual darkness is heavy, almost tangible, and it can affect and bring out the worst in me. Here, more than anywhere else, I am aware of my wicked, fallen nature. By no means do I have it all together just because of the work I do. How desperate I am for Jesus! I must abide in the Vine—He must be my source.

I grab my cup of coffee and open the window shutters. Tangier is a city of hills, and our apartment has a beautiful view overlooking hundreds of homes and apartment buildings, full of people who don't know Jesus. In the distance I can see the Mediterranean and on a clear day, I catch glimpses of the Spanish hills, just eight miles across the sea from our city.

I am currently going through the *Live Dead Joy* devotional. With my journal and my coffee beside me, I begin with my Bible reading— three chapters from the Old Testament, a Psalm, a Gospel chapter, and a chapter from the New Testament. I journal and meditate on the Scriptures that stand out to me. I like to choose one portion of Scripture from my daily reading and read it in Arabic. It may be one verse or an entire chapter. I still have much to learn in Arabic, but I'm amazed at the different perspective that is gained by reading the Bible in a language other than my own. I long for and look forward to the day when Revelation 7 is fulfilled, when multitudes from every nation, tribe, people, and language worship together around the throne.

After my Scripture reading, I read the day's entry from *Live Dead Joy* and pray for the unreached people group mentioned. I meditate and journal an application of the day's devotional. During my prayer time, I pray for my husband, family members, and friends in America. I pray for my leaders and for our supporters who give sacrificially so that we can be here. I pray for fellow workers both in our city and in other countries and for my local friends who don't know Jesus yet. How desperate I am for the Spirit's anointing and empowerment that I may communicate the gospel with boldness, clarity, and understanding. I look across the city before me and pray for my neighbors, that Jesus will open their eyes to see Him. I pray for local believers, those who have counted the cost and are following Jesus. As I write this, a local friend who does not yet know Jesus sent me a text message. I carry my burden for her and for these precious people to the Lord in prayer, "Jesus, open their eyes to see You." I pray and intercede in the Holy Spirit. It is not by my might or language ability or eloquent words (or lack thereof) that they will know.

I end my abiding time with a time of worship and thanksgiving to the Lord. I praise Him for who He is, what He has done, and what He is doing. How faithful He is. How holy and worthy He is. "Praise and glory and wisdom and thanks and honor and power and strength be to our God for ever and ever" (Rev. 7:12, NIV).

INTIMACY WITH JESUS
DICK BROGDEN

"He who abides in Me and I in him bears much fruit; for without Me you can do nothing." –JOHN 15:5 (NKJV)

They called it their "eight to ten." Mom and Dad devoted the prime hours of their morning to lingering with Jesus. They each took their Bible, journal, devotional reading, and a cup of coffee out into the equatorial garden to spend extravagant time with Jesus. You could set your clock by it. This was the foundation of who they were and everything they did. I learned from my parents that the source of all fruitfulness in life is the ongoing presence of Jesus—present through His Word and prayer.

When I was seven years old, my father challenged me to read through the Bible every year. I did so and have continued to do so for the past thirty-nine years. Bible reading and reflection form the core of my "abiding time."

Abiding time is extravagant daily time with Jesus. This extravagant time is the center of abiding. Not legalism, not dry discipline, not manufactured spirituality, but joyous soaking in the presence of Jesus, lavish spending of time with Him who is most precious, Him from whom all life flows. In a world that is over-connected yet lonely, frantically busy yet accomplishing little of eternal value, super-informed but egregiously ignorant on what really matters, abiding gives Jesus the best of our time, in which He leads us to the best of times.

GOD'S HEARTBEAT

The Bible is a missiological masterpiece. From beginning to end, God unveils His grand design to be glorified by every tribe, tongue, people, and nation. Missions is not a New Testament addition. Missions is God's heartbeat from Genesis to Revelation. The Gospel of John is no exception. John is full of non-Jews finding the Savior of the world. John repeats a "sending" motif: Jesus sent by the Father to save sinners, the disciples sent by Jesus to make disciples of all nations.

By the time we get to John 15, Jesus is at the end of His earthly ministry. The teaching of Jesus in John 15 takes place on the night He is arrested in Gethsemane. He is giving His disciples one last charge and pouring out His heart as to what is important. John uses the metaphor of the vine in harvest mode. Jesus is life (the vine), the Father sustains the vine and the vineyard, and the disciples are the branches. Branches are intended to bear fruit (other disciples), and are guaranteed to do so if they abide. Bearing fruit is in fact guaranteed (John 15:5) if the disciples abide.

ABIDING

The Greek word for abiding (*meno*) is connected to the Latin *maneo*—meaning "house." From it, we derive the English word "mansion." Abiding means to remain in one place, at a given time, with someone, to dwell with someone. John uses *meno* to express a reciprocal indwelling: We are in Jesus, and Jesus is in us. We linger in Him and He lingers in us. We live in Him and He lives in us. He is the source of life, He is the sap, and this interaction is both constant and with special times of union. It is both the journey and the destination.

Abiding is elongated, patient waiting in the presence of Jesus. Abiding is extravagant (concentrated) daily times with Jesus and all-day awareness. Abiding is constant communion in the midst of a crowded world and busy life and unique times of sweet, exclusive fellowship. Abiding implies extravagance. When John uses *meno*, there is always a sense of endurance, continuance, tarrying and waiting with expectancy over time.

Men and women of God through the centuries have lived out this abiding truth. There are no heroes of the faith who did not live out this extravagant lavishing of their time on Jesus. When we examine their private lives, we see that they needed to abide for strength and for wisdom. They were addicted to extravagant time in the presence of Jesus because it gave them life and joy and was the only thing that fulfilled them.

Abiding is both active and passive. Abiding is passive in the sense that Jesus pursues us and invites us to rest in His presence. Abiding is active in the reality that the spiritual disciplines position us to receive the life of Jesus—His heavenly sap. Discipline leads us to desire, which matures into delight.

BUILDING BLOCKS

There is no standardized formula for abiding, but Scripture and the biographies of men and women through the ages point us to two non-negotiables: the Word of God and prayer. Extended daily time in the Word and in the presence of Jesus through prayer are the basic building blocks of abiding.

Jesus spent close to 90 percent of His life in a village of twelve families, and even His three years of ministry were characterized by time alone with the Father. Moses spent forty years in Midian and had multiple trips to the mountain with God. Paul spent thirteen years in preparation, some of it in the Arabian Desert, and prayed constantly. Adam, Joseph, David, Elijah, Daniel, Mary, John, and others all gave God extravagant time. When we examine the lives of any heroes of the faith, we can see that they lingered daily with Jesus.

David Livingstone, the nineteenth-century pioneer medical missionary, once said, "Shall I tell you what sustained me amidst the trials and hardships and loneliness of my exiled life? … It was a promise, the promise of a gentleman of the most sacred honor. It was the promise: 'Lo, I am with you always, even unto the end of the world.'"

John York, no stranger to pressure, dying too young from leukemia, expounds on Livingstone's thought and reminds us, "There is no 'Go' without 'Lo.'" First we are called to Jesus; He is with us always, and we with Him, then we go to the uttermost parts and pressures of the earth. At Livingstone's death, his body was found bent in prayer, kneeling at his bed. His Bible was open to Matthew 28. In the margin was this small notation: "The word of a Gentleman.[2]

Mary Slessor was a fire-filled Scottish redhead accustomed to fighting thugs in Dundee with her fists. She went to Africa and fought slave traders and baby killers, giving her life to the Calabar people and fighting for the rights of Africa women. She lived for forty years in a mud hut, and thousands of Africans mourned her when she died in 1915. Her African name was "Mother of All Peoples." Mary cultivated a lifelong habit of chatting with her heavenly Father out loud and incessantly. It was Slessor who coined the phrase, "God plus one are always a majority."[3]

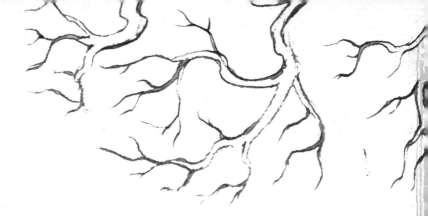

Arab, Moroccan of Morocco

(14,448,000; 0.01% EVANGELICAL)

Jesus told us to pray that the Lord would raise up laborers (hard workers) for the harvest fields. Pray that God would raise up missionaries from all over the world to plant the church together among the Moroccan Arabs (Matt. 9:37–38).

STOP TWO

A Walk Through Tunis

Tunis, the capital of Tunisia, is both the focus of the country's political life and the center of its commercial activity. In the suburbs of Tunis lay the remains the ancient city of Carthage, which hosted many of the North African Church Fathers including St. Augustine, Cyprian, and Tertullian, who played a major role in the development of Western Christianity. Today, the population of Tunisia is nearly 100 percent Muslim, including the largest people group, the Tunisian Arabs.

A WALK THROUGH TUNIS

O ur guest landed two days ago and now that she has adjusted to the surroundings, she's ready to explore. Chatting before her arrival, I discovered that she loves history and current events, exotic food and coffee. We have all of that in Tunis. Nearby Carthage holds history of the early Christianity, and more recently the protests in our own city sparked the Arab Spring. And then there's the Arabic coffee and local foods, no Starbucks or McDonalds to be found here.

"Where would you like to go first?" I ask.

"Take me to your favorite place," she answers.

"I know where we're going to start then."

"It's Sidi Bou Said," my husband cuts in. "It's always Sidi Bou Said."

"Yes, it is," I laugh. Sidi Bou Said sits on a hill overlooking the sea and the rest of Tunis. It is the old part of the city as the capital has extended its way up over the years. "It's beautiful up there. It has an old town feel to it, but it's absolutely amazing. At night it's beautiful with all the city lights, but during the day you'll see the Mediterranean, all gorgeous and blue."

We set out, navigating Tunis' light rail system and make our way there. "This place looks familiar," she says, as we get closer. "I feel like I'm in a wall calendar. You know the ones that feature cities on the Mediterranean?"

"Yep," I laugh, "this part of the city is a tourist destination. All the buildings are white with blue window shades and blue trim. That's probably what looks familiar to you. This area is also famous for its doors. They have some of the most uniquely colored and shaped wooden doors here. It's pretty common to see pictures of them everywhere."

We get off at the Sidi Bou Said stop and head for the streets closer to the sea. I want our guest to take in this view straightaway. As we reach the edge overlooking the sea, she says, "OK, you win. This is beautiful. The water is so intensely blue." I patted myself on the back.

"Anyone interested in some coffee?" my husband asks. We're all in.

Along the way, men are selling souvenirs to tourists. We pass shops and booths full of paintings, pottery, clothing, birdcages, and a wide assortment of trinkets. At the top of the hill is a coffee shop. There are men sitting outside, all facing the street watching the people walk by. We get our coffee and find a table near the front so we can also watch while we chat.

"How often do you come up here?" our guest asks.

"Not too often, but more often than not, if that makes sense," says my husband.

"We'll come with friends at night or visitors like you to have coffee and tea, and just talk and hang out, when there are fewer tourists around," I said. "I have a friend who lives up here and we go up on her roof at night and drink tea and stare at the city lights.

"My closest Tunisian friend and I come up here to hang out, too. I met her on one of my first visits to the city, before I moved here. She was not a Christian at that point, still Muslim, lived with her family. She became a believer about six months after I moved here. Her family kicked her out. The only thing she had was her backpack; her dad took her papers, ID card.

"She stayed with me that night. I did my best to make her feel at home, offering what I saw as basic things like shampoo and hair products. She cried and said, 'No one has ever let me use their stuff like this.' Our friendship solidified in those moments. She stayed with me briefly until the Western family she lived with came back to the country. When they moved, she and I became roommates.

"She had many ups and downs with her family. They wouldn't speak to her for a year. She fully embraced Christianity from the start and shared her faith with everyone around her. She was not afraid; she had no fear of authorities as her father worked for the government. What she didn't understand until later is that her dad was getting pressure about his daughter becoming a Christian. He, in turn, put pressure on her. Eventually they resolved things.

"She worked really hard and never once compromised her faith. She got a job at a school and received many promotions. She shared with the people around her, including some radical people who threatened her, but she led many to the Lord. Authorities interrogated her, wanting her to sign papers, denying she became Christian and become Muslim again. She wouldn't. They asked why, and she shared the gospel with them."

"What a great story," our guest said.

"Sorry, it was long," I apologized.

"No, it was perfect," she said. "I loved hearing it. Most of the stories in the States are doom and gloom, hate and violence. This is a story of salvation and perseverance." She turned to my husband, "How about you? Any good stories?"

"Nothing like that one," he replied.

"Tell the one about the sheep," I said.

"Oh, man. It's not as inspirational as yours."

"It's a good picture of the culture here, though," I said.

"OK so I have been working with college students here," he began, "and there was one guy that I would meet for coffee. He was a very devout Muslim. The end of November that year was Eid, or the Feast of the Sacrifice, where Muslims remember Abraham's willingness to sacrifice Ishmael. My friend invited me to join his family for the celebration. We left at 6 a.m. for the suburbs and upon arriving they lead me to their formal guest room with a couch and TV. They turn on the TV and let me sit there for a couple hours while they prepare the meal.

"Eventually we go outside. I see the sheep there ready to slaughter and a grill about the size of a cereal bowl with a small pile of coals. Some families have the butcher come to the house or just buy the meat but this family was very traditional and they slaughtered the sheep right there. It was a total of seventeen minutes from a live sheep to being grilled on this tiny grill.

"As their guest, they gave me the first piece of meat from the grill and proceeded to grill one piece at a time. The grill was so small you would get one piece of meat every 20 minutes. Then they tell me that they have a special piece for me – the tail – but thinking about it later, I think it was a slice of the brain. It was mushy and not good, but it was their way of honoring me so I ate it."

"Her story was inspirational but yours was highly entertaining," our guest laughed. "It reminds me of stories from my crazy family."

"It does, doesn't it?" my husband replied. "One thing that always pops into my mind is that the people here are just like everyone else I've lived around my whole life. When I first moved here, I thought of them as a completely different people, as if they were people I could never relate to. One day walking down the road, I started looking at faces and imagining them going to work or home to family. I would see man in a suit and realized that he was probably working a 12-hour day to provide for his family. It was then I could relate to them as people. Where first I saw foreigners, now I see neighbors."

"OK, you redeemed yourself in the inspirational category, dear," I said. "For myself, I have discovered that people are really friendly and outgoing. They are open and share things with us. As Westerners, we will be told more personal things than they would tell their own family."

"Why is that?" our guest asks.

"It's part of culture," I replied. "What someone wants to share might not be acceptable to a local person or family member. A local might make them feel shame for saying it. But since the people here think that Westerners can do whatever we want, they think we are less likely to judge them."

"Or they think we don't have any morals," added my husband.

"Or that," our guest and I say at the same time, and laughed.

"Thank you so much for this. I have loved it all: the view, the coffee, the conversation," said our guest. "What's next?"

"Food," my husband says. "Sheep tail, probably."

EXTRAVAGANT DAILY TIME WITH JESUS
WILMA GLASS

When I was a little girl growing up in a Christian home, I learned the Sunday school song, "Read your Bible, pray every day, and you'll grow, grow, grow." I believe it—and my husband Pete and I practice it. Through our thirty-five years of marriage, we have made Bible reading and prayer the two bedrock essentials of our Christian walk.

Two Bible verses highlight the importance of Bible reading and prayer. The first is Matthew 4:4 (NKJV): "Man shall not live by bread alone, but by every word that proceeds from the mouth of God." We hear so much today about the benefits of healthy eating. Excellent spiritual health requires determination and discipline, too. Pete and I try to take time every morning to read and discuss Scripture together.

Psalm 119:97–104 (MSG) sums up our love for God's Word: "Oh, how I love all you've revealed; I reverently ponder it all the day long. Your commands give me an edge on my enemies; they never become obsolete. I've even become smarter than my teachers since I've pondered and absorbed your counsel. I've become wiser than the wise old sages simply by doing what you tell me. I watch my step, avoiding the ditches and ruts of evil so I can spend all my time keeping your world. I never make detours from the route you laid out; you gave me such good directions. Your words are so choice, so tasty; I prefer them to the best home cooking. With your instruction, I understand life; that's why I hate false propaganda."

Word breaks are more important to us than coffee breaks. We were recently at the site of ancient Caesarea, a town in Israel midway between Tel Aviv and Haifa. It was a great time for a Word break. We read the story in Acts 10 where Peter preached to the house of Cornelius at Caesarea. Earlier this year, we were at Saint Paul's Bay on the island of Malta—time for a Word break! We read from Acts 27 and 28, the story of Paul's shipwreck on Malta.

The second verse that guides our abiding time is 1 Thessalonians 5:17–18 (NKJV): "Pray without ceasing, in everything give thanks; for this is the will of God in Christ Jesus for you." Constant prayer with thanksgiving is God's will for every follower of Christ. We begin and end our days with prayer, including large doses of praise and thanksgiving for all that God has done. I often start my day with music and some "worship aerobics" to get my heart really pumping for God. Then, throughout the day, we continue to pray about everything (Phil. 4:6).

"Pray without ceasing, in everything give thanks; for this is the will of God in Christ Jesus for you."

— 1 THESSALONIANS 5:17–18

PLANTING THE CHURCH
PETE GLASS

Pioneering is following the example of Paul: "It has always been my ambition to preach the gospel where Christ was not known" (Rom. 15:20). Pioneers are propelled by possibility. They are always looking ahead, thinking about "out there," just a little further. Paul's conception of frontier missions was one of the constantly pressing beyond where the church was established to places where there was no witness to Christ.

Some imagine that the work of taking the gospel to the ends of the earth is just about wrapped up. Nothing could be further from the truth. More than 40 percent of the people groups of the world are still considered unreached. The Great Commission to make disciples of all nations is still in effect. And since there are thousands of nations—ethno-linguistic people groups—who have never heard of Him, every Christ follower should pray that God would not only make all of us evangelists among our own people, but also that He would raise up from among us pioneers to take the gospel where it has never gone before.

I lived in Dallas for two years while studying Bible and theology at Christ for the Nations Bible Institute. While living there, I worked as a waiter in a chic downtown Cajun French restaurant. Six of the other waiters were Moroccans. I soon learned from them that all Moroccans are Muslim—or so they thought. I grew up in Sheboygan, Wisconsin, and lived there from birth until I went away to college. I had never met a Moroccan and knew nothing at all about Morocco or Islam. But working in that restaurant, the Moroccans and I became close friends. I would often see them slip out to a side room near the restaurant kitchen, where they would kneel together in a line to do their prayers. I grew curious and was soon reading everything I could get my hands on to better understand the faith of my new friends.

My wife Wilma and I began to spend more time talking and reading about Islam, Muslims, and North Africa. We began to dream about visiting Morocco someday and started looking for opportunities. Little by little, we were lifting our eyes to the fields, and in the days that followed, we both began to feel that God might be calling us to live and work there. Eventually, we contacted our missions sending agency and explained that we believed God was calling us to North Africa, specifically to Morocco. I asked if they could put us in touch with one of their missionaries working in the area. Their answer: "We have none."

Not long after I made that phone call, the Iran hostage crisis took center stage in world news. For 444 days, from November 1979 to January 1981, Islamist militants held fifty-two Americans hostage inside the U.S. embassy in Tehran. For the first time, we were exposed to images of chanting mobs of Iranian Muslims shouting "Death to America!" President Carter called the hostages "victims of terrorism and anarchy." More than once during that time, we asked God, "Are you really sure you are calling us to work among Muslims?" Looking back now, we can see how God was opening our eyes to a people and a part of the world we previously knew very little about. He was enlarging our vision of the harvest fields.

John 4 records a teaching of Jesus that reveals great insights for pioneers, especially the idea of lifting our eyes and looking on the fields. While His disciples are away searching for food, Jesus strikes up a conversation with a Samaritan woman at a well.

First, you need to know that Samaritans were literally despised by the Jews. Tensions between the Jews and Samaritans dated back well into the Old Testament period. Jewish and Samaritan religious leaders taught that it was wrong to have any contact with the opposite group, and neither was to enter the other's territories. So you can imagine the disciples' surprise when they return with the food and find Jesus talking with a woman— in itself a cultural taboo—not to mention that she is also one of those detestable Samaritans.

After her encounter with Jesus, the woman leaves them and her water jar and goes back to her town to tell everyone, "Come, see a man who told me everything I ever did. Could this be the Messiah?" (John 4:29). The people flock out to see for themselves.

Now with the Samaritans encircling them, Jesus speaks these words to His disciples: "Lift up your eyes and look on the fields" (John 14:25 NASB). The fields in this case were clearly all the Samaritan people surrounding them. Maybe it was scary. I'm sure the thought of Samaritans being including in the harvest plan had not yet crossed the minds of the disciples. Jesus a few lines down in the text, we read in verse 39, "Many of the Samaritans from that town believed in him," and again in verse 41, "And because of his words many more become believers." For Jesus' Jewish disciples, it must have been a stretch to lift up their eyes toward the Samaritans and to see them as being included in Jesus' harvest plan. I'm sure the disciples were blown away as they witnessed so many Samaritans believing in Jesus.

For many Christians today, the thought of moving to an Arab country to live among Muslims so that they might hear the gospel is also quite a stretch. It was for us. But this is what pioneers do. So here's the point. Lift up your eyes today and take a fresh look at the fields. Ask, *Where are the unengaged, least-engaged, and unreached fields of our world? What is there no church?* The Arab world is made up of 300 million people, and very few pioneers are on the ground engaged in the world of proclaiming the gospel and planting the church were it does not exist. Ask God to help you lift your eyes for a fresh look at the peoples of the world who are waiting to hear the gospel for the very first time. It's their turn.

PRAYER FOR UNREACHED PEOPLES

Arab, Tunisian of Tunisia

(10,345,000; 0% EVANGELICAL)

A person is saved only through the knowledge of his sinful state and the subsequent repentance and turning to Jesus. Pray that the Tunisian Arabs would feel and know the burden of sin and come to Jesus for forgiveness and salvation (Matt. 11:28–30).

STOP THREE

A Walk Through the City

With the fall of Muammar Gaddafi, rival governments and militias
sought control of Libya. As these rivals vied for power, the Islamic State
established itself along a strip of the Mediterranean coast. A new unity
government arrived in the capital in 2016, but it faces resistance from
hardliners of the rival groups. Who will govern Libya—if Libya can
indeed be governed—is an open question. Welcome to our new normal
in the Arab world—instability. And unstable Tripoli, Libya's capital,
is one of the least reached cities in the world.

A WALK THROUGH THE CITY

B oom! Every day sounds like the Fourth of July here. It's either fireworks or gunshots. Now it only takes me a second or two to decide which kind of explosive I've heard. Those were fireworks. Yes, in the middle of the day. Libyans shoot off fireworks anytime, even during the day, even though no one can see them, just because they like the sound. Boom!

How it all feels normal to me now, I can't really say. It just does. It's life here in Tripoli, I guess. Maybe it's a combination of all the sounds, day in and day out; you just kind of get used to them. I mean, I hear yelling all the time and I don't think anything of it. People just yell when they talk. It's not because they're super angry (at least not usually)—it's because they're just loud and animated. Then there are four mosques near our house which makes the prayer call sound four times louder, and there is Arab music and Qur'an chanting coming from everyone's radios and TVs. After a couple years, all the noise piles on top of each other, and it becomes the backdrop of life.

And life here feels pretty normal. I feel safer in Tripoli than I thought I would. Before we got here, lots of people told us we probably wouldn't feel safe. I think my parents and my brothers and sisters would tell you they're surprised by how safe they feel. It's definitely God with us, though the heavily armed military and checkpoints around town maybe help. Where we live is very saturated with military right now. The new government just moved into the naval base nearby—it's about a quarter mile from our house—and they literally arrived by boat. (It's kind of weird and cool that what Americans hear about in world news actually happens down the street.)

One of my favorite places to hang out is here by the water. I can see the Mediterranean from my house, but I love to explore and climb these rocks at the beach. That pier goes pretty far out into the sea. Look! Watch the fishermen out there right now. The waves are huge today, and when they hit the pier wall, the spray goes up over the wall and drenches everyone nearby. There goes one…. Yes! It's an awesome sight. What's not so awesome is this smell. It smells like trash and fish—and not always fresh fish. And look over there! It's the spot where all the big ships come in and out of the port, their long, loud horns among the list of many sounds here.

We always see families together here at the beach. I guess that's a lot like back home. They go to the parks as well. The weird thing about the parks here is that we can't actually play on the grass. There is very little grass around, so if the grass happens to be especially nice, then we can't play on it. We're just supposed to sit and look at the very nice grass. That's how they enjoy their grass. My favorite park is called the horse park. A horse track runs around it where they race horses sometimes. Families have picnics there, and I've seen adults exercising. Also, the slushies there are really good. (Maybe that's why I like that park so much?)

Slushies at the park sound pretty normal, right? OK, let me tell you about a kind of Libyan food that sounds less normal. It's called *bazeen*, and it's the most traditional dish we've had here. Imagine a giant ball of playdough in the middle of a tray covered in gravy. All around it are meat, vegetables, and boiled eggs. Sounds good, right? Maybe. It gets better. You take some bazeen, or the playdough, with your fingers and mash it until it's the right consistency. Just like playdough. Then, with the mashed up bazeen, you scoop up the other stuff around it with your hands and put it in your mouth. Your fingers and the bazeen become a spoon. Or a shovel. Maybe I didn't describe it very well, but it's pretty good. And potentially very messy. I guess this is the only time it's OK to play with my food. I won't tell you if I love it or hate it, but I think you should just try it before you leave.

We don't eat bazeen very often. Most of the stuff we eat is pretty normal, like pizza, kebabs, Turkish food, and gelato. It didn't take us long to find our favorite places to eat, and it didn't take our favorite places very long to recognize us. The pizza guy knows our weekly order and the butcher always knows what we want. He comes out of his shop to greet us if we don't come in. Our fruit guy knows us all by name, and he always asks about my older brother who is away at school. How cool is that? I really like that guy. The waiter at the restaurant where we go every Friday after church saves bottle caps for me because he knows I collect them. I like that guy, too.

We like hanging with kids in our neighborhood. My brother and I ride bikes with the other boys and play soccer. These guys are pretty competitive though, and the rules are very loose and always subject to change, so some days it takes a lot of patience for me to keep playing. We still have fun though. Maybe they'll come around later so you can meet them. We can go up to the roof to jump on the trampoline with everyone. Yes, I said trampoline on the roof. Look, all rooftops here are flat and most everyone uses them as another floor of their home. So our roof is like a backyard, which just happens to have a trampoline on it. To everyone around us, it probably looks pretty funny to see all us kids bouncing in the air above the roof.

There is so much other stuff I want you to see in Tripoli, stuff you'd never heard about on the news. I like it here. I like my Arabic teacher. I like the dirt roads that feel like mazes. I like randomly finding Mountain Dew and Cheerios at the store. I like watching all the young Libyans take selfies. This is home for me now. And I like knowing that my family and I are here to tell these people about Jesus.

EXTRAVAGANT DAILY TIME WITH JESUS
JOY HAWTHORNE

If I set the foundation for my day in the morning, I know I can be a stepping-stone, someone that God can use. I *want* to start my day with that focus, so I try to have my abiding time before the day gets moving. Right now, I don't have a set amount of time for abiding, but I spend at least a half an hour in one place and then keep going throughout the day.

In my abiding time, I read God's Word. For the past year, I've been using a reading plan, and while I don't think I'll always use it, for right now, it works. Because I know others are doing it, it keeps me accountable. There are other times when I focus on shorter portions of Scripture. It's easy to read the Bible just to get through it, but sometimes it's good to just slow down and go deeper. I also like to read a Psalm each day. I read it out loud as a prayer to Jesus before I do anything else.

Honestly, sometimes I forget to pray. I want to grow in this area though, because I know prayer is where I get closest to God. Something I've done in the past is a prayer journal. The way I express myself is through writing, so for me it's a way of worship. In the journal, I write down things going on in life and my praises to Jesus. Sometimes I just say I need Him and ask for His help. I found that when I say what I feel to Jesus, I find answers—well, because He is the answer.

I also try to read devotionals. These don't usually take a lot of my time, but they're valuable. I know I have a lot to learn. These devotionals don't replace reading the Bible or actual experience with Jesus, but I enjoy and benefit from other people talking about their walk with God. I have always loved to read, so for me it's choosing to read books that challenge me and help me grow.

I don't want abiding—something meant to give me life—to become dry and empty, so I try new things. I commit myself to doing something for a certain period of time and find out what I learn about God along the way. For example, every day for two months, I wrote about who God was to me, something different each day.

I have four siblings, and time away from everyone isn't always easy to find, but when I have the chance, I take it. I love to go up on our roof. There's a little room up there where I can see the city and ocean. I pray, listen to music, praise, read my Bible, watch the sunset, and write. I love to go up there to get away from whatever I've been doing and spend time with Jesus. Up there, it's just Jesus and me. Up there, I find myself being refreshed and inspired to go on.

Jesus has become my safe place. When stability is not present in life here, I can lean on Him. When friends are not constant, Jesus is. He knows what I need and provides everything. Jesus is enough for me. Yes, I'm a teenager, but I'm not empty-headed like some might think. I really don't want to be empty at all. That's why I keep coming to Jesus for all that I need, for all that I am. I keep taking another step. I keep trying again. I go outside my comfort zone and trust Jesus to do the work, and then I come back to Jesus to be filled with Him when I feel empty inside.

Through all the doors I walk when I visit neighbors and friends or when I meet people at the grocery store, I want to walk with Jesus. I abide in Jesus first to be close to Him, to hear what He is saying, to follow what He is doing. I abide in Him to learn to love the unreached people I'm called to serve and to be truly effective to bear fruit while living here. Abiding in Jesus daily gives me purpose because now my life is no longer about me—it's about Him.

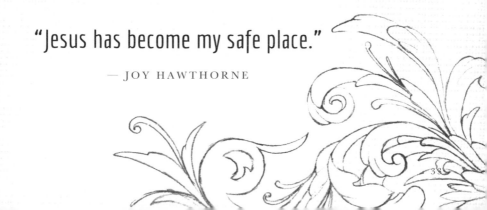

"Jesus has become my safe place."

— JOY HAWTHORNE

33

PEOPLE WORKING TOGETHER
MARK RENFROE

I really don't understand it. God seems to be up to something great. We talk about how hard the work is and how it will cost us deeply to see Jesus glorified among the 400 unreached people groups of the Middle East and North Africa, but new missionaries keep coming. They're young men and women, mid-career professionals, and even those who have retired but want to finish well. They want to do something that will have an eternal impact for the King and His Kingdom.

THE REASON FOR TEAM

The idea of team sounds like heaven, but it can feel like hell. It brings out the best and the worst in us. It's God's instrument to conform us to His image. Often, we wind up on a team with personalities that grate against us. God uses team for planting the church, but also for refining the worker, and the process of team is a glorious deconstruction. I cannot think of one person who has gone through the process and not been refined by God.

We have (at least) four reasons to do church planting in teams. First, it is the biblical model. We tend to read Acts and point to Paul's leadership ability. But as we read his Epistles, we realize how many people ministered with him. Sixty-four people are mentioned as co-laborers between Acts and the Epistles. Locals joined ministry teams that represented many cultures and were sent out together. Second, like reproduces like. Individuals reproduce disciples. Communities reproduce churches. Rarely do we see individuals reproducing whole communities. Third, teams just make sense in organizational structures. Missionaries tend to rotate on and off the field. Teams provide an approach to maintain longevity in a location. Finally, teams offer a multiplicity of gifts for the work. Missionaries are each gifted in their own way. As an individual, a missionary might flounder in pioneer church planting, but on a team he can still make a huge contribution to the church planting work. Team gives a missionary who is not apostolically gifted an apostolic expression.

THE MEMBERS OF TEAM

We want to have teams that are multi-national, multi-agency, and multi-generational. In time, we want all our teams to have these three components. To be multi-national is to reflect heaven: "There before me was a great multitude that no one could count, from every nation, tribe, people, and language, standing before the throne and before the Lamb" (Rev. 7:9). Multi-agency shows humility, that we need whole body of Christ to do the work of church planting.

A majority of our team members today are young and full of energy and excitement, which we love. Being multi-generational gives us depth and experience. Older people tend to lower emotional temperatures (i.e. my kids may argue in front of me, but they won't in front of their grandparents). Multi-generational teams have openers and closers, young people just starting their missionary careers and long-time missionaries joining later in their careers. Teams will also have people coming mid-career, leaving a job back home to bring their experience to the field.

One young couple in Egypt tells me that being on a multi-generational team gives them the chance to learn from those who've already pioneered. They see team as a way for each new generation of missionaries to have the chance to start on the field at a greater depth than the previous one because of shared wisdom and experience. Dick and Jennifer Brogden poured their fifteen years of experience from Sudan into this couple in just two and a half years, which expedited the learning process for them. The same has happened in multiple places across the Arab world with different veteran and newcomer partnerships.

Then there's the couple with thirty years of experience in Latin America who recently transitioned to a team in the Arab world, excited about using their last years of ministry in a strategic effort to take the gospel to people with no access to it. Their move to North Africa was a challenge. Ministry here is 180 degrees different from ministry in Latin America and learning Arabic later in life, not all that easy. But their biggest concern was actually working on a team. When they started overseas ministry thirty years ago, "team" was not a popular concept in their circles. But they say the team concept has been a blessing and great learning experience. Though they have more experience on the field than most all of their team members, they know they are novices when it comes to working with Muslims in the Arab world, and while they have a great deal to offer the younger team members, they are learning with them at the same time. They don't lead the team, but their team leaders lean heavily into their hard-earned experience. This couple models humility as much as anyone I know.

THE NEED FOR TEAM

The work in our part of the world is pretty straightforward. God has called us to make disciples among every people group, and we believe the best way to do that is to plant churches—that is, house churches with the DNA of multiplication. We don't want to simply see churches planted. We want to plant churches that will plant churches so more and more disciples can be made and the knowledge of the glory of the Lord will increase among the unreached.

Our focus is to take the gospel where it does not exist, which isn't hard to find our context. We still have entire countries with fewer known followers of Jesus among the local population than you have fingers on one hand.

So how we do this is pretty simple because the Bible seems pretty clear. The early disciples went out in groups to plant the church. They were armed only with their love of Jesus and the power of the Holy Spirit. We do the same. We are committed to community, and we focus on doing our work in teams. Dozens of new volunteers join one of our four training teams every month and learn language, culture, and tools for planting the church. But more importantly, they learn what it means to abide in Jesus. Jesus told His disciples that if they abide in Him, they would produce an abundant crop of new believers (John 15:4–8). Abiding is key. Jesus is everything.

The Rashaida of Saudi Arabia are waiting. The Bedouin of Jordan are waiting. The Berbers of North Africa are waiting—and so are the nearly 400 other unreached people groups scattered across the Middle East and North Africa. It's time for teams to reach them.

Arab, Libyan of Libya

(1,868,000; 0.2% EVANGELICAL)

False religions and deceptive ideologies have blinded men and women throughout the world to the truths of the gospel. Please pray that God would unveil the cross and would remove the veil from the minds and spirits of the Libyan Arabs (2 Cor. 3:16–17).

CAIRO, EGYPT

STOP FOUR

A Walk Through Cairo

The largest city in the Arab world, Cairo holds the ideological heart of the Muslim world. In Islamic Cairo stands Al-Azhar University, Sunni Islam's most prestigious university, which serves as the center of Arabic literature and Islamic learning. From Al-Azhar Islamic scholars render edicts (or fatwas) for the world of Sunni Islam. The Arab Spring brought change to Cairo and to Egypt. Many protested for democracy in Tahrir Square, followed by an election in which the Muslim Brotherhood won a majority of seats. A short-lived victory, military coup ousted the new president one year later, followed by another election. Cairo and Egypt live in a measure of stability with an understanding that the next wave of change could arrive any time.

39

A WALK THROUGH CAIRO

I take a step outside the door of my language school, and the sounds of the city I love surround me. I remember back a couple years ago when my wife and I arrived in Cairo. All the people, all the noise, the activity overwhelmed me. Walking down the street was sensory overload. Now all of these are what I love about life here.

I turn towards home and make my way through the streams of people on the sidewalk and along the street, my feet crunching on sandy concrete and broken roads. Sometimes the transportation of my own two feet is the quickest way to get from point A to point B in our corner of Cairo, even with all the weaving between parked cars and trading sidewalk for street. I dodge cars like a pro now. One of the first lessons everyone learns here is that once you start to cross the street, you commit to it. Because every car, bus, bike, and donkey cart has already committed to going around you. A slight pause or second guess does no one any good.

Large busses and taxis fly by as I reach the other side of the street, and the sound of honking horns fills the air. It's a sound I once found a little annoying; now it's like a strange music to my ears. The cars, trucks and busses use their horns to speak their own language. I've learned that horns are integral to driving in Cairo. I heard a story about some friends who were in a taxi on the way to the airport when the taxi driver pulled over and told them to get out. They were confused because the taxi seemed to be running just fine, but he refused to take them any farther. Turns out, he said his horn stopped working and he wouldn't drive without it! So they found another taxi and continued on their way. Life in Cairo!

I reach our (mostly) quiet neighborhood street and turn towards home. If there are no men on the street, I can reach my building in about three minutes. But if there are men outside, all bets are off. And I quite enjoy it. Each man I pass wants to shake my hand, kiss me on both cheeks, and proclaim peace upon my family and me, and if I'm by myself, they will ask about each member of my family. Now Egyptians love babies, so if my little one is with me, every friend and every stranger will hug her, hold her, and speak blessing over her. My daughter's name means "light" in Arabic, and she truly opens doors for us to share about the Light of the World.

I have to tell you, the birth of my daughter was not only one of the greatest moments of my life, it was one of the greatest ways my wife and I could display our love for this city and these people. From the moment we learned about the pregnancy, we had no doubt that our baby would be born in Egypt. Though I admit, when she arrived two weeks early and our entire team was out of the country, we faced a moment of fear because everyone that we wanted at the hospital was gone. Suddenly feeling alone in Cairo, we were challenged to be even more dependent on Jesus, and that was the beginning of the Lord showing us how He would use our family to love our neighbors. In that moment we needed them, and one by one our hospital room filled up. Our Egyptian neighbors, teachers, and friends surrounded us. We were never alone. There is nowhere else in the world we would have rather become first-time parents and raise our children. We learned our life here is not a sacrifice, but a joyful privilege.

I walk up to my building and find my neighbor outside. We exchange greetings, and he tells me a joke. It's the same joke he tells me every day, but he laughs just as hard every time. It's absolutely wonderful. I love how simple and joyful the people are here. Every interaction is filled with laughter and jokes. It seems like Egyptians always have a joke or story to tell, and they'll talk with anyone willing to listen. Still, for all the joy and laughter this city and people bring us, there is much that breaks our hearts. Devout Muslim men sit on street corners holding their prayer beads and reciting the Qur'an, unwilling to hear about or even talk about Jesus. An old woman with flies swarming around her begs God for mercy and asks passersby for coins. Young men fight loudly in the street, sometimes to the point of pushing and hitting each other.

The physical needs here are clearly evident—but how much more the spiritual need! There are five thousand registered mosques in Cairo from which the call to prayer goes out five times each day. That means every day twenty-five thousand denials of the deity of Christ are proclaimed over the forty million people in this city, including my very good friend Mohammed, a passionate and articulate young man whose greatest desire is to spread Islam. He is studying *douaa Islamaya* (an invitation to Islam), and he eagerly shares his faith with anyone who seems to be a prime candidate for Islam. We talk about the holiness of God and the love of God. He is so confused about the Trinity and how I could believe in three gods, and he wonders why such a powerful, almighty God would die on a cross, making Himself so weak. I love talking with him about God's requirement of atonement for sin and about God's love, a love so great that He chose to die in our place, making a way for us to be in His presence. Mohammed is always so eager to meet and discuss these ideas with me, and I pray that they become more than just ideas to him, but truth and life.

The need for Jesus here is inescapable and overwhelming—but the harvest is ripe. We're often asked if the Islamization of Egypt is a drawback to people receiving the gospel message, but we find that these actually make people more open to the message. It seems that as the oppression of Islam becomes more severe in this part of the world, the questions about God become more prevalent and hearts more open.

EXTRAVAGANT DAILY TIME WITH JESUS
DICK BROGDEN

You believe in a financial tithe. All your resources belong to God, and you return to Him a portion of what is already His. What about your time? Does it all belong to God? Should the principle of tithing apply to your time? How extravagant are you toward Jesus with your time? Do you lavish time on Jesus? Do you give Jesus the most energetic and focused times of your day? Or do you tend to give Jesus the crumbs of your schedule? Here is what I enjoy doing in my abiding time.

PRAYER

I have never been particularly good at sitting and praying. I need to pace, move, pray out loud—otherwise I get distracted; so I start my abiding time with a run—literally. I run two miles and then walk home. As I walk, I pray. I usually pray through the points of the well-known acronym ACTS.

- **Adoration** (15 minutes): I praise Jesus, love Him, exalt Him, worship Him for who He is, who the Bible says He is.
- **Confession** (15 minutes): I confess my sin and failures. I also confess who God is. I recite the Apostles' Creed. I often do this out loud—confessing to the powers in heaven and to the others on the street, the wonders of who Jesus is.

- **Thanksgiving** (15 minutes): I thank Jesus for His created world, for friends, family, favor, health, blessings. For the Holy Spirit, for the prevailing blood, for the Word, for all He has done and all He is.
- **Supplication** (15 minutes): I make my petitions known.

At the end of the ACTS prayer (and sometimes in the middle), I will also:
- Pray in the Spirit (Eph. 6:18), allowing the Holy Spirit to pray through me and build me up in the inner person.
- Wait quietly on the Lord, trying not to say anything, but just to listen to what He wants to say to me.

BIBLE READING

For my time in the Word, I daily read six chapters: three chapters from the Old Testament, one from the Psalms, one from the Gospels, and one from the Epistles. I mark up my Bible like crazy, make notes in the margins, and try to summarize one key thought on top of each column. These usually take about an hour.

SUPPLEMENTAL READING

I often read from a devotional or spiritual classic. Francois Fenelon, Oswald Chambers, Richard Foster, and C. S. Lewis are all favorites.

MEMORIZATION

I try to spend about five minutes a day memorizing Scripture.

PRAISE

I end my time by banging out hymns on the piano or strumming good old 1950s choruses on the guitar. I sing and express my adoration to Jesus in somewhat off-key enthusiasm.

THE WHOLE CHURCH, THE WHOLE GOSPEL, THE WHOLE WORLD
DICK BROGDEN

M y wife and I don't feel apostolic. We don't wake up and see super-apostles in the mirror as we brush our teeth. We don't feel like we're in the same league as Paul. We don't feel like opening up Asia Minor for the gospel, enduring shipwrecks and stoning, rebuking foolish Galatians, standing up to religious councils, evangelizing Caesar's house, shaking snakes off into fires, singing hymns in prison, or happily having our heads chopped off.

When we get up in the morning, we feel tired, overwhelmed, unable, and feeble. We open our door and look at tens of millions of Muslim Arabs in our city, despair that they march unwarned into hell, and think there is no way we can make even a tiny gospel dent in a seemingly impregnable community. And then we look over our shoulder and see there is no one standing in line behind us. We are the ones God has in this place and in this moment, and the Holy Spirit must and will help us to live and minister in apostolic function—even if we feel nothing like Paul.

Apostolic function proposes that every missionary (and even every Christian) can live for the glory of God among all peoples. Not all missionaries or Christians have the same gifts, but all our gifts combine to see Muslims come to Jesus. My hours of email and administration contribute to God's glory. My wife's hours of shopping, cooking, hosting, serving, and washing dishes contribute to express the heartbeat of God. My team member who coordinates our home school co-op labors faithfully so the missionary kids' parents can preach the gospel to a Muslim family who has never heard of Jesus. My team staff leader oversees our logistics and banking, so the whole team has time for language study and empowered proclamation.

Our team all participates in the big picture by some daily, hidden, practical role. None of those roles in isolation are the gospel or apostolic, but taken together and working in harmony, we in community function apostolically that the gospel can be preached fully in this Muslim city. When one Muslim in our city comes to Jesus, we all have a part in that salvation—every mom who spent four hours of her day in the kitchen, every teacher who helped a missionary kid with math, every administrator who spent four hours on budgets, emails, and strategic planning, every logistician who fixed cars, houses, and plumbing. One person physically prayed with the new convert, but we, all together spiritually, walked that new brother or sister into the family of God.

THE INDIVISIBLE SPEAR

One way we illustrate apostolic function is through the image of a spear. The spear reflects the work of the mission—the collective call of the Church moving towards the target of planting the Church where it does not exist. A typical spear illustrates how the work of missions can operate.

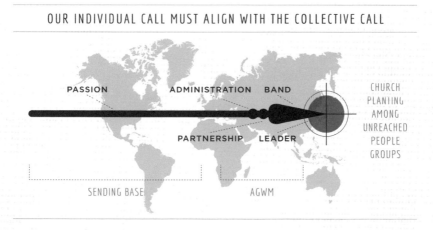

OUR INDIVIDUAL CALL MUST ALIGN WITH THE COLLECTIVE CALL

At the point of the spear is the Church being planted in an unreached people group. It embodies apostolic leaders of church planting teams—men and women with the calling and gift of being an apostle, leading others to pioneer the church. Joining them on the spearhead are multi-gifted team members who engage in church planting among the unreached. Their involvement in discipleship, training, translation, social concern, member care, and Christian education are part of the larger strategy to develop a robust, fully indigenous church among a group with little or no access to the gospel.

Also on the spearhead are missionaries whose ongoing work strengthens the growing indigenous church and encourages others to work for church planting among the unreached. We call this *apostolic partnership;* these missionaries are not on a church planting team but they mobilize funds, people, and prayer for the advancement of the church everywhere—with an emphasis among those not yet reached. A fourth segment of the spearhead includes *apostolic administrators*—missionaries who serve in administration, leadership, and strategic development. Every missionary on the spearhead needs to be able to draw a straight line from their particular call and personal obedience to the collective call and obedience we all partner in—that is, planting the Church where it does not exist.

But a most critical part of the spear is the shaft. A spearhead without a shaft becomes just a few impotent inches of metal. We call the shaft of the spear *apostolic passion*. It refers to pastors, laymen, church volunteers, mission committees, donors, intercessors, senders, and mobilizers—men, women, and children who live their lives for the glory of God in their home countries for the sake of reaching the unreached people of the world.

Every missionary and every partner belong to this indivisible spear; they each have a role in apostolic function. Through the spear, every Christian can discover how his or her calling aids the whole Church taking the whole gospel to the whole world.

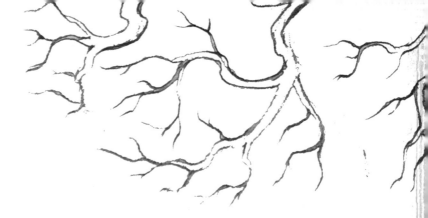

Bedouin, Eastern Bedawi of Egypt

(902,000; 0% EVANGELICAL)

The Bible says that God has given His followers a spirit of power. Pray that believers among the Eastern Bedawi Bedouins would be set free from a spirit of fear and would boldly proclaim the truth of the gospel (2 Tim. 1:6–8).

STOP FIVE

A Walk Through Amman

Welcome to Amman, the capital of Jordan and the residence of King Abdullah. Amman is a city rich in biblical history. In the days of King Saul and King David, it was the capital of the Ammonite empire. Later, it became part of the Roman Decapolis (or Ten Cities) in which Jesus ministered. The city was initially built on seven hills but now spans across nineteen among which you will find Jordanian Arabs.

A WALK THROUGH AMMAN

H ere, time is flexible. There is always time for everything in the life of a Jordanian. Me? I'm the one who lived and died by the clock in America. There, time is a structure that makes things happen. That isn't a bad thing—it's just different here. Jordanians do value time, but in a very fluid way. The way they view time with relationships and with people is just different than Americans. The adjustment wasn't easy, but I've grown more comfortable with living less by the clock.

Today is one of those days—a day for me to wander. It's nearly noon, and I set out to walk through the Citadel near the center of Amman. I like to visit there from time to time—it has the best views of all parts of Amman and is a great place to pray for the city. It's not far from my flat, and I enjoy the walk. I'm not in a rush.

The Citadel represents the military, historical, and spiritual center of the city. It has ruins from Roman, Byzantine, and Islamic eras—and they say, maybe even the Bronze Age. Amman is one of the oldest continually inhabited cities in the world. In the Old Testament we know it by the name Rabbath-Ammon in the kingdom of the Ammonites (Deut. 2:37), and we read about it in the story of King David, who sent Bathsheba's husband Uriah the Hittite to his death on the battle's front line, maybe even attacking this very hill (2 Sam. 11).

On my prayer walks, I follow a certain route through the Citadel. It's a pattern I learned to pray through the various parts of the city and for its diverse people. I start at the Byzantine Church, built in the 4th century A.D., when Christianity became the religion of the Roman Empire. Here I pray for a new passion among the nominal Christians who live in the city. I look east from the wall by the church to East Amman, the home to many refugees of Palestinian, Iraqi, and Syrian origin. The Palestinians have been here for more than sixty years. Although integrated into society, many still call themselves refugees and live in one of thirteen camps around the country. I pray that they would find a new identity in Jesus and realize earth is not their only home.

I head north along the wall and look over the tightly packed buildings. There are hundreds of homes representing thousands of lives. I can see my building and think about my neighbors. I think about my friend Yusur who has the most beautiful green eyes. Yusur was a timid Iraqi bride, slender and pale, who came to Amman with no friends and no family. We quickly connected and developed a friendship despite our different backgrounds. She had a passion for life despite the fears of war and an arranged marriage. She is one of the kindest souls I have ever met. I say a prayer for her and wonder if she might meet me at a coffee shop later on.

Over the buildings I see the flag of Jordan waving proudly. I've heard its one of the world's tallest flagpoles—over 400 feet tall. It stands on the grounds of one of the royal palaces, Raghadan, where the late King Hussein is buried. King Abdullah is a 43rd direct descendant of the prophet Mohammed. His wife is Kuwaiti-born Queen Rania, who is from a Jordanian family of Palestinian origin. They have four children. I lift up the royal family today and pray that King Abdullah will receive God's wisdom to make decisions for this country.

Passing through the ruins, I walk toward the west side of the Citadel. I see towers rise above the horizon: hotels, office buildings, apartments, and malls. This is where much of the new development in Amman is happening and where the king's vision to transform a desert kingdom can be seen. I pray that people would not be captured by the god of materialism, but would be set free by the one true God.

The Roman temple of Hercules lies ahead. It was the ancient spiritual center of the city, built in the 2nd century A.D., and housed the statue of the deity. It is believed that a much older site of worship existed here, during the days of the Ammonites. The history of religion in this city moves me to declare the Jesus is Lord here. He is the Lord of this city. From the temple I catch a good view of downtown. I see the busyness of the markets surrounding the Husseini mosque, Amman's oldest, and on the hilltop across stands the Abu Darwish mosque. I pray for an outpouring of the Spirit over each person— the shop owners in the market, the mothers and children walking down the street, and the religious leaders of the mosques.

In the museum behind me are fragments of the Dead Sea Scrolls. These prove the accuracy of the modern translations of the Bible. One of the lies people here believe is that the Bible has been corrupted—they grow up believing this as fact. I pray that the lie will be broken in this people and they will have a hunger to study the Word of God.

On the way home, I pass the ancient Roman amphitheatre. Built in the 2nd century, it holds around 5,000 people and was the center of entertainment in the city then called Philadelphia, one city of the Roman Decapolis. For the equivalent of twenty-five cents, I can visit the ancient site. My favorite time is in the morning when things are still peaceful and quiet. From the top level, I can see the entire city start the day, and the air is filled with the smell of coffee as the spice grinders begin roasting their batches of coffee.

I decide to call Yusur as I walk home, hoping she'll be able to meet me for coffee later on. We can sit in our favorite window with our lattes and watch the Bedouin shepherd walk his fifty sheep across the street from one vacant lot to the next looking for grass. I love how surprising this place can be—keeping its traditions while pushing towards modernism. It truly is the place where time is flexible—where it can stand still even as it moves forward.

EXTRAVAGANT DAILY TIME WITH JESUS

MIRIAM DAVIS

I'm pulled out of my dreams by a distant sound. I roll over and glance at my clock. 4:45 a.m. I hear it again, the sound of the *ethaan*—the early-morning call to prayer. My apartment is near the top of one of the city's many hills, and on the next hill over, just across from my bedroom window, the minaret of a mosque stands tall and calls out clearly.

I roll back over and doze for a few minutes. My phone soon vibrates next to me. It's my own call to prayer, of sorts. *Jesus.* I whisper His name as I sit up and pull back the covers. The call to prayer sounds again. *There is no God but Allah and Mohammed is his messenger.* The blatant denial of my Lord's deity called out by speakers, and I whisper His name again. *Jesus.*

My bed is comfortable, and my flesh doesn't always win the battle. Some mornings, the act of getting out of bed is inspired by one simple thought: *Do it today.* I've learned that not spending time with Jesus today is one step in not spending time with Him tomorrow. I know that if I don't abide in Him, I will not bear fruit. I'm disappointed to think of the days that felt like a loss because I wasn't connected with Him. Yet He has always been present, drawing me back into deeper times of intimacy. And every time I choose to get up when I need to, set aside distractions and focus on Him, I find joy and fruit.

My abiding time has changed over the years, and I like the flexibility of discovering what works in each season. I have found that for me, the elements of prayer and reading the Bible are non-negotiable. Other disciplines of journaling, memorizing Scripture, speaking specific passages aloud, and simply being silent before the Lord are all ways that I connect with Him.

I sit down with my cup of coffee and open my Bible. When God promised to provide manna in the wilderness, He gave Moses specific instructions. "The people are to go out each day and gather enough for that day" (Exodus 16:4), He told Moses. The provision came daily. It was impossible, except in preparation for the Sabbath, to gather extra—and those who gathered none went hungry that day. My Bible is the bread that sustains life in the wilderness. Yesterday's Word isn't meant to sustain me today, and if I don't partake, I will go hungry. The Bread is free for the taking—this is daily intimacy.

I close my Bible and spread out a blanket on the floor. I sit in the solitude of the morning and talk with the Lord. I hear the second or third call of the *ethaan* in the distance, and I'm grateful that He's looking for my heart, not my performance. I talk to Him about the previous day and I renew my surrender to Him. I ask Him to remind me to abide in Him moment by moment. I listen to what He wants to speak to my heart, and sometimes I smile from His encouragement and sometimes I cry from His gentle rebuke. He is always there, calling me to deeper, daily surrender.

I pray for those I will interact with today: language helpers, neighbors and friends I made through teaching English. The call to prayer reminds me most of the Muslims around me are deeply committed to good spiritual behavior. It reminds me that, in itself, the act of waking up early to pray has no eternal significance unless my heart is connected with Jesus. For my neighbors, the call to prayer five times a day is not a call to *abide*. It's a call to an attempt to please God through obedience and sacrifice. For me, there is a different call to prayer, a call from my Master: "Come to me. Abide in Me. Follow Me." Like to my neighbors, I "make it [my] aim to please Him," but I do this knowing that *already* "God made Him who had no sin to be sin for us, so that in Him we might become the righteousness of God" (2 Cor. 5:9, 21). I can do nothing to please Him on my own. I can only accept His invitation to come and to abide. I have no guarantee that I will abide tomorrow, but if tomorrow I determine that I will "do it today," the pattern will continue and I will continue to bear fruit.

UNDERSTAND THE CULTURE
MIRIAM DAVIS

B ob has never been to the Arab world but has influenced work among Arabs in ways he doesn't even realize. I first met Bob, my adopted grandpa, because he is a dedicated lifelong learner.

As I prepared to go to the mission field, I worked two jobs to save as much money as possible. My weekend job was at a local coffee shop. Saturday mornings in small town Minnesota were always quiet. I opened the shop, prepared some baked goods, and did a little cleaning until my one faithful Saturday morning customer came in for his raspberry white chocolate scone and 16-ounce Highlander Grogg (which I brewed every Saturday because I knew he'd come in). He always ordered them to go, but once we learned one another's names, his coffee went cold because we stood at the counter and chatted until the next customer came.

I call Bob a lifelong learner because every Saturday when he returns home with his coffee and scone, he goes down to his basement where his television is and inserts the next DVD in his current series of university courses, which included subjects like art, science, history, and economics. Three times a week, Bob keeps his appointment with himself and his DVD course.

Bob's commitment to lifelong learning inspires me, but not because he pursues academic knowledge. His discipline in academia is just one reflection of his passion for learning. Bob has influenced me, and in turn influenced the Arab world, because he loves to learn *from me*. I am decades younger and have so little understanding of life compared to my wise adopted grandpa. Yet whenever I'm America, Bob makes sure we find a few hours every month to share a meal so he can ask me question after question about my life, my experience, my faith, and my work.

As Bob gives me his full listening attention, my trust for him grows. I share not only my experience, but also my heart. I know he understands because he has listened for so long. I ask him questions, too, and he shares his wisdom. It's Bob's willingness and desire to listen to and learn from me that opens the door for him to speak into my life.

Lifelong learning has many facets. Live Dead missionaries are committed to learning and growth far beyond their first term (which is largely dedicated to language and culture acquisition). Members of church planting teams are always looking to learn more about the people groups they serve because greater understanding feeds passion and strategy. However, learning *about* a people group isn't the key to the door of gospel proclamation; learning *from them* is.

One morning, I showed up to an Arabic lesson and found my regular tutor was sick. The school had arranged a replacement for me that day, a young man named Khalid. Anytime I have a new tutor, I ask them to share a bit of their life story with me. Khalid talked and I listened intently. After he shared his story, he said he'd like to make a recording on the Arab Spring. History and politics aren't my strong suit, but I've discovered that Arabs place great value on knowing and understanding context. They have a shared context that they've built from years of experience, and I need to learn that context in order to best see how the gospel can reach each individual.

We started the recorder and Khalid began talking to me about history, then politics, then his religious viewpoint. After he finished talking, Khalid and I listened to the recording together, and I asked questions about words and concepts I didn't understand. "Now it's your turn to talk," Khalid said. "What do you like to talk about?" I told him that I love talking about language learning and about the *injeel*. "Ok, that's a good idea," he replied. "Let's discuss religion."

"Ok, that sounds good, but that's a wide subject. Is there a specific question you could ask me?" I asked him. I wanted to see how interested Khalid was in hearing.

"Tell me," Khalid proposed, "when Christians say that Jesus took away your sins, what does that mean?"

I began walking Khalid through the Old Testament stories of sacrifice, something I had practiced going through on my own and with other tutors. I told him about the requirement for sacrifice for the atonement of sins. We came to the New Testament and opened the Scripture to John 1:29, where John declared Jesus the Messiah to be "the Lamb of God who takes away the sins of the world." He listened and asked me to help him download the Scriptures in Arabic to his phone.

I never had another session with Khalid after that, but I'm confident that the Spirit planted seeds of truth in his heart. The door was opened for me because I showed Khalid care by listening. Attentive listening opens the door for proclamation.

Back home, Bob keeps on learning from his courses, and he keeps on learning from me. I want to be like Bob by learning more information about the culture I'm living in, but also by taking intentional time to listen and learn from those around me. Arabs are waiting for someone to come alongside them, understand them, and share truth in a way they can comprehend. Let us be those people.

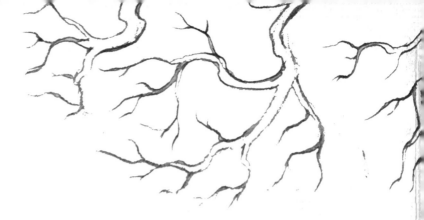

Arab, Jordanian of Jordan

(1,121,000; 0.3% EVANGELICAL)

God's Word is so much more powerful than anything people can say; it is a mighty lion that needs to be unleashed. Please pray for the Word of God (in written, oral, musical, and dramatic forms) to be translated and to rise among the Jordanian Arabs (Isa. 55:10–11).

STOP SIX

A Walk Through Damascus

Damascus is the world's oldest continuously inhabited city. It holds great significance in the life of the Apostle Paul where on Straight Street he regained his sight and was baptized. In the wake of the Arab Spring, uprisings against the government began in 2011, leading to a civil war that divided the country and displaced half of Syria's twenty-two million people, many of whom are from the country's largest people group, the Syrian Arabs.

A WALK THROUGH DAMASCUS

I used to live in Damascus. During a recent visit with my neighbor, I discovered that her sister and children had just arrived from there. The situation is so dangerous there now that the woman's husband sent them away. My heart sank into my stomach. Each day as the unrest continues in Syria and fighting in Damascus, I get more concerned for my dear friends, the Muslim family that lived across the hall.

I love that family. They adopted me into theirs while I was there. Where most Syrians seemed afraid of me at first, this family opened their arms to me from the beginning. Their door was always open to me, and I was over there four or five times a week getting help with my Arabic. This family was my family. If I had to go to the airport, they took me. I played with their two kids. The wife taught me how to make Arab food. We chatted for hours and hours; they were fascinated by America, and I wanted to know more about Arab culture. I even served as the chaperone for the man's teenage nieces. And now I wonder where they all are.

I revisit my favorite stories of them, to keep my mind on pleasant things. There was the day they took me to the market. I got ready and as I waited for a knock on my door, I started playing my keyboard. I didn't realize that they were out in the hallway and could hear me. I stopped playing, wondering what was keeping them. After a couple minutes they knocked. "You stopped playing," they said. "We never heard music like that before." They had been just outside the door listening to me. But the best part of the story is that for months I struggled to construct sentences and carry on conversation in Arabic. As we walked the market, I told them about the music I was playing, why I was playing it and for whom I was playing. That night I shared the entire gospel with them. It was the first time I ever shared the gospel in Syria and the first time ever in Arabic. It was divine intervention because it was so far beyond my Arabic abilities to share all of that. I got home and thought, "What in the world was I even saying?"

I remember my Christmases there. My second Christmas in Damascus, my mom sent a care package of decorations, including a stocking for my door, which led them to ask about the strange sock. They wanted to know all about Christmas, so I explained the whole Christmas story about Jesus. I asked if they had any questions. "Yes, what about the fat man and little people and gazelles?" I smile now, but my response then was, "Really? That's your question?"

Life in Damascus was often like that: amusing, surprising and interesting. I found one of the best places for amusement and interest was in the Old City at the Souk El-Hamidiyeh, a huge market and one of the oldest in the world. It is a labyrinth of interesting things that spreads out for miles in every direction. I wandered through that market for hours shopping and meeting different people. I wonder what it looks like now, and how many people are still wandering its alleyways. I remember the man in a fez hat near the entrance to the market. He carried a giant pot of coffee on his back and poured it from the pot into little cups for people to drink. He clinked the cups together to get people's attention. I was never a customer; the idea of communal cups kept me away.

I could have two different experiences at the market depending on how I dressed. I only spoke in Arabic, so it mattered whether my hair showed or not. As soon as they looked at me, they knew I was not Arab. If I had my hair completely covered, they assumed I was half-Arab or very fair because they could not see my hair. In that case they would treat me like any other Arab. I got better prices, and the men never looked at me but we did bargain. When my head was uncovered, they dealt with me very differently. I could be friendlier with my head uncovered, but I was also harassed more. I normally only went with my head uncovered if I wanted to practice my Arabic. I had some fun conversations that way. There were a few shop owners who let me sit and talk with them. Once a week, I stopped to visit and have tea with one particular shop owner. All the items in this man's shop were handmade in Syria, and he would tell me where each thing came from and show me old money from different places. He was so kind and so interesting.

His shop was right in front of the Umayyad Mosque, which is the one of the holiest mosques in Islam and where Muslims believe Jesus will return. Covered in my long polyester coat and hijab, I visited the mosque often. This mosque has several distinct areas in it. I talked to people visiting the tomb of Saladin, the champion of Muslims during Crusades. The head of Hussein, the grandson of Mohammed, is there. I sat for hours with women who were distraught and needing God to intervene. In the main room is a shrine with the head of John the Baptist, and I went to the back of the room where the women were and discussed the Quran and the Gospels and John the Baptist with them, and inevitably, no matter how I timed it, the call to prayer always sounded. The entire room stopped to pray, heads to the floor, and I watched them go through their prayers.

This was my life in Damascus, one of the oldest continually inhabited cities in the world. Imagine—a city with people living in it for 5,000 years or more. When I lived there, the city seemed to straddle the 14th and 21st centuries. I bought my vegetables from a cart pulled by a donkey, ridden by a man talking on his cell phone. Now I read that there were attacks near the Umayyad Mosque and see images in the news of empty streets, shops closed, and buildings bombed in different Damascus neighborhoods. I pray for my family. I might have no way to reach them, but I trust God knows how.

EXTRAVAGANT DAILY TIME WITH JESUS
EVA BRIDGES

My husband will tell you that he never speaks to me in the morning before I've had my coffee and my Jesus time. I'm simply not a nice person before Jesus washes me of myself and pours His Spirit over me. So I get up early every morning, make a cup of French press coffee, and then go over my Scripture memorization cards. I try to memorize a new verse each week in English and Arabic.

I then read a portion of Scripture. Because I am a creative person, I've learned that one-year Bible plans and devotionals simply don't work for me. I need variety and spontaneity to keep my relationship with Jesus fresh. Sometimes I study a single person in the Bible for several weeks. Sometimes I focus on one verse, meditate on it, and then write in my journal. Sometimes I read an entire book of the Bible at one time. I usually end this time by reading authors such as S. W. Tozer, C. S. Lewis, or John Eldredge.

After reading from the Word, I move to my prayer time. Because my brain wanders, I try to focus my prayer time. I've developed a weekly schedule so that I'm sure I pray for all those in my life each week. However, I do allow my mind the freedom to express my prayers in a variety of ways. Sometimes when I pray, I am inspired to write poetry. Other times, I lie on my face in my prayer room as I intercede for those around me. Sometimes I sit and stare at the maps on the wall showing countries we've lived in and listen to God's heart for the people in those areas. Although I am disciplined in having this time with Jesus, my abiding time is fluid. I generally don't worry about the time and rarely look at a clock. I simply continue in this time of prayer until I feel released in my spirit to begin my day.

One thing I have discovered is that I can't survive throughout the day on just one block of time with Jesus. So at some other point in my day, I spend time basking in His presence. Some days are busy, so this time may be only a few minutes. Other days are more flexible and free and I have the luxury of spending another thirty minutes with Jesus. Most of the time, this means sitting at my keyboard and playing whatever my fingers decide to play and my voice decides to sing. Sometimes, though, I write or sketch or just look at my flowers on the balcony. At other times, I go on prayer walks by myself or with a likeminded friend. This time is simply a time to love Jesus and allow His love to pour over me.

For me, abiding isn't only about the time in the morning when I pray and read. Abiding is a lifestyle. Abiding is praying for the lady who cuts me off on a busy street. Abiding is praying for the guy who is saying inappropriate things to me. Abiding is Jesus living through me. At times, I fail miserably and allow my flesh to overtake the situation. But at other times, I know the Spirit of God is at work in me, so He can work through me.

"Abiding is a lifestyle."

— EVA BRIDGES

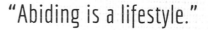

LIVING WHERE YOU MINISTER
EVA BRIDGES

When we first moved into our apartment, many of our neighbors were concerned about having Americans in the building. They've seen American television and movies and assumed our lives would be similar. They worried about whom we might bring into the building and what that would mean for their own families. They decided that they would be nice to us, but not really get to know us.

We, however, were committed to living in community with our neighbors. We desired to live openly with them. We made intentional decisions about where we would live, how we would furnish our home, and how we would dress. Each decision was made so that those in our community would feel comfortable in our home and see us as moral and good people.

From the very beginning, we visited each neighbor with a plate of American goodies. I learned a long time ago that chocolate-chip cookies will soften anyone's heart. Several times a week, I set aside time for visiting with the ladies in my building. We talk about life, they teach me Arab dishes, and I teach them American desserts. They help me with my Arabic, and I help them with their English.

Now I consider many of them a part of our family. They know they can drop in anytime, and we can do the same. Our lives are intertwined as we live together in community. These neighbors share their needs, and we commit to pray for them. And because we live so closely together, they often comment on our commitment to God and our moral lifestyle, which gives us the perfect opportunity to share about our love for Jesus. Life in community creates space for the Holy Spirit to work in the hearts of those around us.

COMMUNITY AND THE CHURCH
We see in the book of Acts a picture of believers meeting in homes as they discover together what it means to be followers of Christ. We see them conducting spiritual aspects of life together through prayer, and then we see

them living life together through the breaking of bread. They were a close-knit group of people. They were in each other's lives every day. They went to the market together, they ate together, they prayed together, and they fasted together. Everything they did was together. Life is meant to be lived with others.

However, what's amazing is that they weren't exclusive. "And the Lord added to their number daily those who were being saved" (Acts 2:47). It's easy to stick with your group. These are people you know. These are people who know you. You're comfortable there. However, God's love is not exclusive. His grace is for all.

Community is not a feeling of belonging. Community is a deep unity. Community is each person knowing his or her place. It is watching the smile on Jesus' face as we all work together to create seemingly impossible things we can only imagine.

Community is sharing together. We should be drawn together as believers because of God's grace through Christ (Phil. 1:7; Rom. 6:3–4). We have a common inheritance as sons and daughters of the Most High that should lead to worship and prayer together.

Community is sharing outwardly together in common service. Grace is not only for believers. God's love is not exclusive. The truth should be given to others. It is through outreach that the community of believers helps to reconcile to God those far from Him.

COMMUNITY AND A PERSON OF PEACE

The church has worked for centuries to create methods to reach the lost. We've gone door to door sharing the gospel. We've built tents and preached the Word. While those are valid means, Jesus instructed His followers to locate homes and men of peace. This is no easy task—which is why He stresses the importance of prayer beforehand.

Jesus asked His followers to do this because building community with a person of peace goes further than just that individual. Jesus was starting a new movement. To do so, He needed as many people to hear the truth as possible. So, He developed a system whereby His followers told one family and then that family told people in their community, and so on.

Fatima is my person of peace. Honestly, she's the last person I would have chosen. A preschool teacher, she doesn't have an influential job. She's not a leader in the community or even the leader of our building. She's not even his wife. Instead, she's his daughter. But she is the one whom God has placed in front of me. We meet together to talk as she's discovering that she's a sinner in need of a Savior. We've developed a trust, and now she comes to me to share her concerns and needs. She's looking for a listening ear and the knowledge that someone is praying for her.

What I find most interesting about our relationship is that although she has not given her heart of Jesus yet, she is constantly bringing other people to my home. She has a network of young women who are desperate for relationships, and Fatima sees me as the answer to that problem. I pray that Fatima discovers the truth, but until that time I am thankful for her connections and willingness to bring me into her world. In a place where everything is done in community, I trust that one day she and many of her friends will find the truth together.

Your person of peace has a network of others who need to hear the truth as well. In effect, the more time you spend with your person of peace, the more opportunities you have to share the truth with him or her. Then, your person of peace can share the truth with those in their circle. In essence, you'll be affecting the lives of countless people as you invest in your person of peace.

Arab, Syrian of Syria

(14,448,000; 0.01% EVANGELICAL)

God promised to pour out His Spirit on all flesh, men and women, young and old, rich and poor. Please pray that God would pour out His Spirit on the Syrian Arabs, that they would see dreams and visions of Jesus and that they would be powerfully saved and empowered to be His witnesses (Joel 2:28–32).

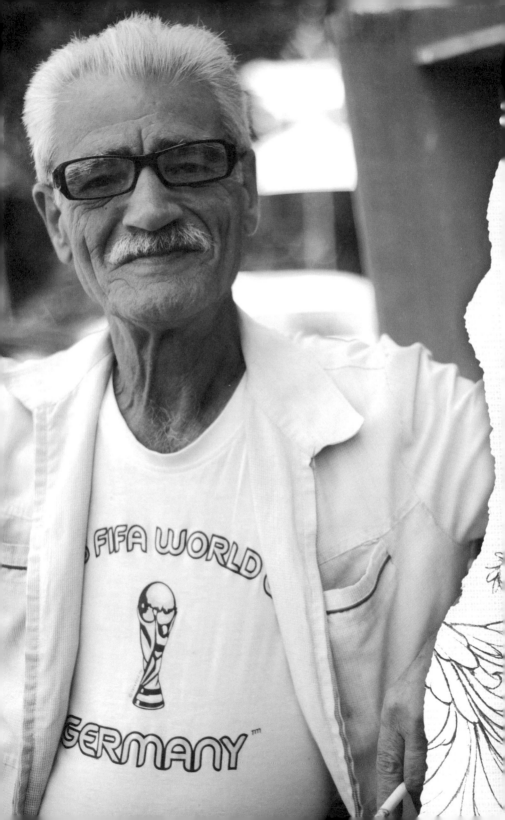

A Walk Through Baghdad

*Baghdad became the capital of Iraq in 1921, though the city
dates back to 762. The second caliph of the Abbasid Empire,
al-Mansur founded Baghdad for its strategic location on the west
bank of the Tigris River. It grew to be one of the largest cities
in the world as well as a center for international trade and a
famous center of learning. Baghdad declined with the caliphate
in the thirteenth century and the eventual arrival of Ottoman
Empire but grew once again with establishment of the country
of Iraq in 1921. Today, the city remains a strategic key to the
region—it is the largest Shiite city in the Arab world, and Iraq
has the second largest oil reserves in the world.*

A WALK THROUGH BAGHDAD

O n my way to church, I pass houses surrounded by high cement walls with razor wire stretched across the top. The sight doesn't surprise me really; I expected to see things like that. But as I continue on my way, I see busy restaurants, moms and kids at the park, people at fruit stands, pharmacies and grocery stores doing their daily errands as I make my way through the city. I've discovered something about Baghdad; it's like pretty much everywhere else in the world—despite challenging circumstances, life goes on. The people who have chosen to stay (or have to stay) here don't stay shut up in their homes. They go about their normal lives.

Arriving at the church, the smiling faces of my friends greet me. They are so warm and welcoming to me—a new face, an American face. I find that Iraqis are generally open to foreigners, and while many of them don't have much opportunity to learn English, they are especially appreciative of efforts in Arabic (like my feeble ones). These people are incredibly hospitable and generous. It's impossible to visit someone's house without them serving tea or coffee and so many treats.

My friends and I make our way to the building across the street that the church uses for its weekly ministry to kids and their mothers. I so enjoy my time with these women in their black *abayas* and headscarves. I love hearing their stories; they make me laugh and make me cry, sometimes at the same time. Most recently, the stories of newer refugees from Mosul and villages in the north have struck me hard. A mother of three showed me pictures of their house. "We have no idea what's become of it now," she said. The family received news late one night that ISIS was coming. Within two hours the entire village fled, taking whatever belongings they could carry. And these were the lucky ones. Many pushed out by militants had everything confiscated, escaping only with their lives and the lives of their children. I am so grateful for the church here that serves so many of them, providing them with housing and gifts of food.

As part of the ministry this week, our pastor's wife comes forward and we all listen closely as she shares truths from the Bible. The children never cease to amaze me. They jump in with questions like, "Why did Jesus die on the cross?" Hearing them even confess this truth with their mouths overwhelms me. Perhaps one of the most surprising things here is the openness that many Iraqis have to the gospel. "Shiites love Christians," an Iraqi pastor once told me. I discovered that Shiites tend to be less strict than their conventional Sunni counterparts, following tradition more than religious texts, and they are more open to sharing their hearts with anyone who will listen.

After our ministry time, my friends and I go to restaurant down on the river for kebabs. The kebabs here are the best—perfectly seasoned meat, grilled crisp. Our table is covered with salads, local bread, and hummus. Everything is so delicious. Evening has fallen, and I make my way home. In this new light, the city takes on a different beauty—the streets and restaurants light up, families are out eating ice cream, young men drink tea in the park. Traffic slows a few times as cars pass checkpoints where guards wave us through.

I look forward to tomorrow. I have plans to visit my favorite place in Baghdad—a well-known market in the inner area of the *Karrada* neighborhood. It's always as full of people as it is history and life and color. Shops are organized by what they sell. I usually start by the small clothing shops that blast air conditioning. Out front, sellers have stands with clothes on hangers and shoes on tables. A block down is a road lined with household appliances, both big and small. Walk a few more minutes to find well-lit gold shops with stunning window displays. Dispersed throughout are restaurants and ice cream shops, and the aroma of grilled Iraqi kebab mixes with the distinct smell of the popcorn stand. The two-way traffic is heavy and gets stuck as people look for a parking place. The Shiite call to prayer echoes in the distance—it's distinct from the Sunni call: *I testify there is no god but Allah, and Mohommed is his prophet, and Ali is the friend of Allah.* The call is always heard clearly, but people never seem to stop their errands to acknowledge it.

Oftentimes, I forget where I am. This city looks and acts nothing like the Baghdad I saw on television back home. The car bombings and kidnappings we hear about in America are not as widespread or as frequent as one would think. The friendliness of the people, the amazing food, the activity around the city, and the beautiful river are rarely (if ever) seen in the news media. I guess news broadcasts have no reason to show the rest of life in Baghdad that is relatively peaceful and quiet. Some days I hardly believe that I live in what is considered one of the most dangerous cities in the world.

For as normal as I can feel in this city at times, I know that many hurting people do live here, people thirsty for Living Water. The pain of years of war and instability cause them such suffering. I am so blessed to know my pastor and his wife and their grown children, who together decided that, even when their extended families left, they would follow their purpose here—to lead a congregation to be salt and light to Baghdad. How sweet is their love! How amazing the grace!

EXTRAVAGANT DAILY TIME WITH JESUS
CAROLINE HAWTHORNE

A wise mentor and friend shared with me, "Growth is better watered by meditating upon who He is, than obsessing over who I am not."[4] This has been a timely word for me in a dark place. It causes me to examine where my focus and confidence rest. Never before have I felt so small to the task, so desperate for Jesus, so lacking in nearly everything, than since our arrival here. What a glorious gift! It is a wonderful truth that I am not enough, a genuine relief that I don't need to attempt to be what He is. With my gaze on Him, all striving with the exception of staying close to Him, ceases. For it is when I focus my attention on myself, that things begin to feel as though everything is closing in on me.

A question that has impacted the way I practice God's presence, particularly since our arrival here, is, "Who holds my gaze?" Is it upon Him, on myself, or on what my eyes can see? This awareness of my deep need of Jesus has intensified. The longing of my heart is to live in moment by moment abiding in Christ.

How does this look practically?

I start first thing by getting out of bed *with* Jesus, saying something as simple as "Let's get up now."[5] It reminds my brain that I do not embark on a new day alone. I try to maintain the discipline of time with Him before checking any form of media. I find I'm better suited to respond to others after I first meet with Him. It also keeps my mind from wandering to whatever news I just read. I spend time abiding in His presence through worship, the Word, listening, and prayer. I also redeem the time in the shower by spending it praying in the Spirit. The call to prayer heard multiple times every day is not just for those around us. It is a call for us to pray as well; it's a wonderful reminder of why we are here. I begin to pray, often just speaking the name of Jesus aloud and praising Him.

We set apart time for family abiding, but as a mom, it is critical for me to practice a lifestyle of abiding *with* our kids. I don't leave and go pray—I just pray and praise out loud with them many times throughout the day. While there is much about my abiding that is personal, I try to be very intentional about living it out loud in the presence of our kids (Deut. 6:7, 11:19).

Something key to my abiding has been to remember that it is about the entirety of my day, not only a set time I spend with the Father. Many times each day, there are a few key prayers—most just a few words in length—that I breathe out as often as possible to lift my gaze to Him and put my focus where it needs to be. It may be whispers of love, requests for a consuming passion for His glory or requests for the grace of self-forgetfulness. I have boiled down some longings of my heart to a few phrases that I can breathe out in prayer and praise. They keep my gaze and affections on Christ and take the focus from myself or from what I see in the natural realm. I speak these prayers as often as possible throughout the day.

The darkness that sometimes feels like it's closing in around me presses me toward Jesus—I count it as a treasured gift from the Father. I have never longed for Him more or found Him more precious to me than in this place of immense darkness and instability. Though I have walked with Jesus for many years, I am just now beginning to learn what it means to really trust Him, to be stretched, and to experience a true longing that He be praised by those who surround me. He is worthy of their praise, and it is born out of my time in His presence so that I will be a fragrance to those who are perishing (2 Cor. 2:15) and to those within the walls of my own home. May it be that as we are all pressed, it is the fragrance of Jesus that spills from us.

DEPENDENCE ON THE HOLY SPIRIT
MARK RENFROE

C hristie has been part of a Live Dead Arab World church-planting team for six months. She is frustrated by the aggressiveness she experiences every day on the streets of her city. It appears that she is becoming increasingly negative toward her husband, colleagues, and about life in the Arab world. The excitement she had when she arrived on the field is long gone, and she's wondering if she can make it.

Dear Christie,

I have lived in the Arab world for twenty years, and I still face some of the frustrations you feel. The traffic, the aggressive way people push, the extreme noise of an urban setting, and the outward piety of my neighbors that doesn't seem to affect their behavior wear on me. I get frustrated by the way men look at my wife, daughter, sisters in the faith, and other women on the street. If I'm not careful, I can become cynical and angry, and when that happens, the devil wins. Too much is at stake for me to let that happen. Let me share with you what I do when I see those attitudes and actions creeping up in my life.

The first thing I do is to take the smile test. I know it sounds cheesy, but I simply look in the mirror to see what my face looks like. Is my face soft or hard? When was the last time I laughed at life and at myself? Am I having fun anymore? These may sound like superficial questions, but the one thing I have discovered over the years is that the singular thing people have in common when they decide to leave the field is that they have lost their joy.

I love Galatians 5. In the latter part of the chapter, Paul talks about the "words" of the flesh and the "fruit" of the Spirit. There are no believers in my neighborhood (at least not yet, but we're believing that this will change soon!). Everyone is a Muslim. They are all trying to work their way to heaven. What do you think this produces? It produces the behaviors Paul writes about—impurity, hatred and discord, jealousy, fits of rage, selfish ambition, and dissension, to name a few. Here's the reality. Lost people act like lost people, and the more separated they are from the influence of the Kingdom of God, the more their actions and attitudes deteriorate.

What I have noticed about myself is that I get frustrated and angry when I focus on behaviors. That is when I need to remind myself that Jesus came into the world to save sinners—not to simply clean up their behavior. Jesus is in the heart-transplant business, and sometimes I need to ask Him to work on mine so that I can lead others to Him.

Galatians 5:22 tells us that the fruit of the Holy Spirit is love, joy, peace, kindness, gentleness, etc. Fruit is the opposite of works. Living in the presence of Jesus will produce these qualities in me. Yes, that will make me look very different to my neighbors, but for all the right reasons. When I'm living close to Jesus, the Holy Spirit works like a magnet in me. He restores my joy. And who doesn't want to be around joyful people?

Christie, the naiveté you brought to the field is long gone. The question is, "What will replace it?" Will you live daily in the light of the father and become the spiritual magnet that He desires you to be? Or will you let cynicism and anger take root? As you have discovered, it isn't our love for the lost that sustains us, it's the Father's love for us. I'm confident that you will find your joy renewed and your first love restored as you move toward Him.

Your fellow pilgrim,
Mark

"Jesus came into the world to save sinners— not to simply clean up their behavior."

— MARK RENFROE

Arab, Iraqi of Iraq

(14,148,000; 0.2% EVANGELICAL)

Jesus wants His followers to be one. Please pray that God would unite the body of Christ. Pray that Christians from around the world would work together to reach the Iraqi Arabs and that the Iraqi Arabs would be joined to the body of Christ (John 17:20–23).

STOP EIGHT

A Walk Through Doha

You have arrived in Doha, the capital of Qatar and host of the 2022 World Cup. A country slightly smaller than the state of Connecticut, Qatar is the world's wealthiest nation. Despite its material wealth, it remains spiritually impoverished. The Qatar Arabs comprise less than 20 percent of the total population of their own country, and they are nearly 100 percent Muslim.

A WALK THROUGH DOHA

I walk through the neighborhood, and all I see are walls. Imposing ten-foot walls surrounding huge new well-kept houses and walls around older rundown homes in need of a fresh coat of white paint. Walls are a common theme in Doha.

The modern history of our country, Qatar, is a short one. It has only been in the last 40 years that the people in the villages along the coast moved into city housing. It was then that most of the neighborhoods, like this one, took off. Today the neighborhoods are still changing, much to the chagrin of the locals, who feel totally surrounded by expatriates.

The world resides in this Doha neighborhood: the poor Southeast Asian single men living ten to a room, the Southeast Asian families living three families to a house, the professional Filipinos sharing rooms, the Arab families from other countries in humble apartments like back home, the middle class locals living comfortably in walled houses with extended family, and the wealthy locals in large walled palaces with beautiful green gardens. Doha covers the spectrum of nationalities and societal classes.

I continue in the direction of the local mosque. The large local families inhabit the newer homes I pass; the multiple large SUVs parked out front are a dead giveaway. I see older homes divided into multiple living spaces, including tents in the yard, for the workers from Southeast Asia that cannot afford the high rent. The smell of their Indian and Asian food makes its way to me on the street. I approach the mosque, a somewhat humble structure and the focal point of the neighborhood, where the men go to pray. It has not been as well maintained as some of the houses; it has chipped paint and a crack in the cement of the minaret.

Looking around, there is almost no one else on the street, which sounds odd but is pretty normal. Families are very private, and women are seen as little as possible. I hear children playing behind the walls and some men chatting. Always there is the sound of construction, and I know the call to evening prayer will come soon. With the call to prayer, men will stream out from behind the walls and make their way to the mosque. They don't stop to talk to each other, though I know later on, around 9 o'clock, they will head to *majilis*, a tent in the area where they will sit and talk until late with relatives or a friend that stops by to say hello.

I met one of my own friends at a coffee shop earlier this afternoon. Our families met at the park some time ago, and our friendship formed over a mutual desire to speak each other's language—he wanted to learn English and I, Arabic. We get together from time to time to catch up on each other's lives. One interesting thing I've noticed about my friend and his family is the amount of time they spend together. He and his wife and kids often lunch together and take trips to the park; we even ran into them the other day in a parking lot as they headed to the mall. They act very much like my own family.

What makes this so unique is that according to their tradition, the greater responsibility is to one's extended family—to brothers and sisters, cousins, aunts and uncles, and so on. Much less time is spent with immediate family. Many nuclear families only see each other on Friday, when the man will spend time with his wife and kids. Instead, families here keep a tight social schedule dedicated to extended family—women with their aunts and sisters, men with uncles and grandfathers, and kids with cousins.

My friend does fall very much in line with tradition in other areas. For one, they strictly separate by male and female during any visitation or mixed gathering. When they invite us over, the men are in a separate room from the women at all times, even if it's our entire families visiting. We enter through two different sides of the house, and when the visit is over, my wife and I call each other on our cell phones and meet at the car.

And there's the evening call to prayer. As I watch the men emerge from behind the walls, I think about how each person in the neighborhood is precious to Jesus. Oftentimes, walking through the neighborhood, my wife and I are overwhelmed about where to start. As I pray and think about each house, I ask that the Kingdom of God would extend to each one, that the Word of God would be studied in each one, and that Christ's freedom would be experienced by the many hurting in each one.

Each house, each family, each person has a façade. Women are covered. The men are in robes. Houses are hidden. Everyone gives off the air that they are OK, that everything is fine. And everything is white—white cars, white clothes, and white houses—giving the appearance that everything and everyone in Doha is clean. We know it's not. My wife and I know that everything is not OK; we know people with tragic stories, with hurts and needs. Despite the flashy wealth and fast cars and white robes, we know people who are hurting and walking in darkness.

Despite the walls and the facades, my wife and I choose to look at this neighborhood with eyes of hope. Some days it's not an easy task, but we do it because we know that we serve a Lord who wants to send light into these settings. The reality is that there is no way for us to get behind these 10-foot walls, but the spiritual reality is that we serve the Lord who breaks down spiritual walls. The physical and spiritual walls might be meant to keep us out, but we see God helping to open the doors, and we continue to pray for freedom of these people.

EXTRAVAGANT DAILY TIME WITH JESUS
CATHY STONE

In the morning when I rise, give me Jesus! I heard the words to this song many years ago, and it became the cry of my heart. I grab a hot cup of tea and crawl into my comfy chair. I can be easily distracted so I change up my prayer times. I typically start with praising Jesus and thanking Him for who He is and what He's done. I then read my Bible. I read through the Bible every year but change the translation and the plan each year. After reading my daily plan, I study a specific book of the Bible as the Spirit leads me. I also use a couple of devotionals each day, and I journal my thoughts and prayers as I go. After I read my Bible, I spend time journaling. I love to write His words and promptings daily. My journals have become markers in my journey that remind me of the faithfulness of my God. And who knows, maybe one day someone in the next generation can read them and find Him also.

I then walk and pray out loud and pray in the Spirit for fifteen to twenty minutes. I take time for confession and reflection and ask the Lord to show me what I need to see and do. This is when I pray for others (family, friends, leaders, co-workers around the world). This time varies each day. I pray until I feel the release to move forward. Then I try to sit again and learn to be with Him. (Usually during this time my mind starts making a list of all the things I need to do, so I keep a pen and paper close to write them down. That way, I can stay focused and tend to those later.) After, I work out on the elliptical or walk and pray over a different country and its needs each day. As I finish up my exercise, I listen to a short sermon.

I've realized that what I desire I become—Jesus is my desire, and I want to be like Him. When we started this journey of living dead, I struggled so much with being away from our children and grandchildren. There were days I found myself crying, "I just need to see them and be with them." I would look at family pictures on my wall and think often of them. One day I realized I should have the same cry in my heart to just see and be with Jesus— just because I love Him and want to be near Him. So throughout my day I try to stop and look at Him and just love Him. I sing praises to Him and follow with worship music, but mostly I look for the song that comes from within to offer to Him. In addition to my prayer list of family, friends, the lost, His Kingdom plan and anything else I am led to pray that day, I have wall maps to pray and intercede over as the Holy Spirit leads. I memorize a verse and meditate on it weekly; I place the verses on note cards and tape them around my kitchen so I can study them as I work.

At the end of my set abiding time, I prepare spiritually for the day. I envision myself putting on the whole armor of God, so that no area is left exposed. It might sound cheesy, but I believe when I'm willing to be used, He is willing to use me and I want to be fully covered in Him. I pray that Jesus will give me God encounters as I walk out my door into the city each day, that wherever I go, He will give me eyes to see and ears to hear what the Spirit is speaking (Isa. 33:21). I pray for my new friends, neighbors and those I pass on the street; I ask Jesus to let them hear Him call their name and that truth will be revealed.

For me abiding is positioning myself daily to worship and adore Him. After years of searching, I oftentimes would hear Him whisper to my spirit, "Come closer." Now my abiding time has grown to just being with Him. On the days I can see and hear Him— and on the days I can't—abiding is where I'm learning to know Him. I find that when I abide without hurrying and with desire, I hear Jesus speak things only for me. In the years I spent teaching others about Him, I found myself always looking for a lesson in everything He said to me. Now I realize that sometimes He speaks just to me, for me, just because He loves me.

THE PURSUIT OF HEALTHY LIVING
KEVIN STONE

Three years ago, I was given a great gift. Dick asked me to be his accountability partner. To be honest, I really didn't know what that meant. I thought it simply meant holding one another accountable for our actions. I learned it was so much more.

My wife and I were newly arrived to the field when Dick invited me to this. I barely knew him, but that didn't seem to matter too much to him. The first time we met, he dove right in: "We should be completely honest with one another about our actions, thoughts, attitudes, everything. I'll go first, then you pray for me, and then you go, and I'll pray for you." What happened next shocked me. Because no one has ever been so open and raw with me, especially someone I barely knew. He exhibited an amazing amount of trust in me. When he finished, I prayed for him, and he said, "It's your turn." I didn't say it out loud but I thought, "Yeah, right, I don't even know you." I confessed some things—I didn't want to come across as self-righteous—but I definitely hedged. I did not share everything. He prayed for me, and we set a time to meet the next week.

Our meetings continued on a weekly basis, and Dick (soon no longer a stranger) continued to be completely honest and open with me. Our prayer times grew stronger and trust developed between us. I began to loosen up and became more and more honest and open. After a while, something special developed between us. I found someone—in addition to my spouse— with whom I could be totally vulnerable. I found victory over sins and freedom from self-consciousness. I quit wearing the mask I hid behind.

Dick is the kind of person who likes pushing things to the deepest level. One time he asked if we were being completely honest with one another or if we were still hiding some things. We both agreed that we were about 95 percent honest. So he said, "No more. Today we go to 100 percent. I'll go first." And he did, and then I did. Our relationship went to the next level. Another time he asked if there were any skeletons in our closets that we hadn't shared. I said there was. Again he said, "No more. We are getting rid of those skeletons. I'll go first." He did, and I did. What resulted was an amazing gift, someone who knew everything about me—my sins, failures, hopes, fears, dreams, and insecurities—and he still loved and accepted me.

Accountability is about having someone in your life that you can be real and honest with, someone with whom you can be yourself. It's about having someone who knows everything about you but still loves and accepts you as you are and challenges you to become everything you can be. With him I have nothing to hide and nothing to fear. It has been liberating, empowering, and life changing, and it is the kind of the relationship I think everyone longs for but few ever realize.

THREE CIRCLE MODEL

Accountability between Dick and myself is about transparency in all areas of life: family, ministry, purity, attitude, everything. We use [have used] what's called the Three Circle Model: red, yellow, and green.[6] Green is healthy living. Yellow includes our points of weakness and vulnerabilities. Red is sin.

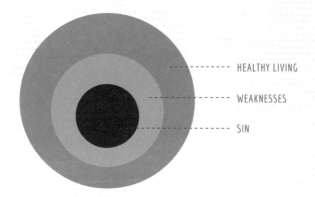

HEALTHY LIVING

WEAKNESSES

SIN

In our accountability we talk about the green circle to focus on healthy living—what things are we doing to stay in the green. We talk about the things that keep us from our weaknesses (yellow) and from sin (red). If we start our meetings with confession in the red circle, that means we've already sinned, so we always aim to push confession out to the green circle before our vulnerabilities and weaknesses have the chance to make their move.

The creators of the Three Circle Model say the circles were designed to create healthy spiritual patterns in life, not to be used for intervention when sin has occurred. Dick and I started to use the model, and it helped us discover what makes us vulnerable (yellow) to sin (red). We could then set healthy standards for living in the green and hold each other accountable to them.

Sin thrives in darkness but dies in the light (John 3:19–21), so when we confess our sins to one another through accountability, sin loses its power over us and we find healing.

Accountability will loosen sin's grip on me, on Dick, and on you. I encourage everyone to have an accountability partner to meet on a regular basis, face to face, to talk about the red, yellow, and green, and to pursue a life of healthy living that honors Jesus.

Every team member in the Arab world is asked to find an accountability partner. For the married ones among us, that means someone besides our spouse. That's why Dick asked me. Finding that mature, same-gender follower of Jesus who is honest, transparent, and with whom it is safe to share and pray is a critical step towards living out our value of accountability.

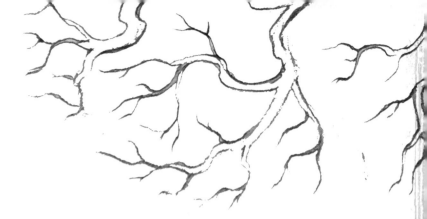

Arab, Qatar of Qatar

(2,256,000; 0.1% EVANGELICAL)

Pray that the hearts of the Qatari Arabs would be like good soil, ready to hear the gospel and respond (Matt. 7:1–8; 18–23).

STOP NINE

A Walk Through Dubai

Welcome to the ultra-modern city of Dubai. Once just a small fishing and trading village on the Arabian Gulf, Dubai is now a global hub for trade and finance. While not the capital of the United Arab Emirates, it does have the largest population of the seven city-states that comprise the country and boasts the tallest building in the world, the Burj Khalifa. Truly an international crossroads, fewer than ten percent of the population of Dubai are Emirati peoples.

A WALK THROUGH DUBAI

M y view of Dubai starts with an elevator ride—from the ground to the 124th floor in just over a minute. The elevator moves so quickly, my ears pop, but the view from this vantage point is worth it. I like my periodic trips to the Burj Khalifa. I can see and remember where I am and why I'm here.

The Burj Khalifa is truly a sight to see. The tallest building in the world is fantastically beautiful. Standing at the bottom looking up, I marvel at the minds that dreamed up such a thing. It's just kind of...mindboggling. And when seen at distance from most anywhere in the city, it looks almost unbelievable, like it can't actually be real. There is nothing in this world—or at least very few things—like it.

Dubai's skyline began to take shape in 1978 with the arrival of the Dubai World Trade Centre, and by the looks of things, I'm pretty sure it never looked back. Only Hong Kong and New York City have more skyscrapers now—I googled it—and all of them built in just a few decades. The architectural designs piling up along Sheik Zayed Road, the main artery through downtown, are immense and imaginative. There are curved and twisty skyscrapers, twin skyscrapers modeled after the Chrysler Building in New York City, and one inspired by Big Ben.

I walk to the north side of the observation deck. From here I see the Arabian Gulf, and just off shore the World Islands, over 300 small manmade islands roughly shaped into the continents of the world. The World, as it's called, was created for luxury resorts and private homes, but was stalled with the global financial crisis in 2008, as was much of the real estate development in Dubai. Recent years have seen the city-state dig itself out of the collapse, but time will tell if the dream of resorts on manmade islands in the shape of the world happens or if the World Islands of sand are just one more sight to enjoy from the air.

I look to the right and trace the streets to find City Walk, an outdoor mall where high-end retail meets street cafes. I often meet my friend Farah there for dessert and coffee. We always skip Starbucks and usually go to Hummingbird Bakery. Now, if Hummingbird Bakery sounds kind of American, that's because it's an American-style bakery started in London and now in Dubai. The British, the Emiratis, and I guess everyone else enjoy American cupcakes. It's just one of many Western chains found here.

Farah and I first met at another café in the city. I was new to Dubai, and she was there by herself, so I worked up the courage to say hello. I had had a couple opportunities to introduce myself to other young Emirati women before Farah, but their expensive shoes, beautiful abayas and headscarves, and stunning makeup intimidated the life out of me. Emirati women seemed to have no use for me. It seems like they have everything they need, and sometimes I feel like I have nothing to offer them. But really I have the One that matters—Jesus. Where Emiratis have every physical and material need met, as Muslims, they lack spiritually—they lack Truth.

I don't know if there was anything special about Farah that led me to her, other than her being alone. I just knew I had to overcome the fear and intimidation I faced so that she could hear about Jesus. I mean, there's no language barrier here; everyone speaks English. So I did it. I introduced myself, and I asked if she was meeting someone. She wasn't. Well, she met me that day and it was not as scary as I had imagined, and she was not intimidating at all. She was friendly. A bit standoffish, maybe, but I heard this can be the case. Emiratis, the locals, aren't quick to open up to expats like myself. For the longest time, expats only stayed in Dubai for a couple years before they returned home, so I get that. Why would you trust someone who only appears to be in your city temporarily on business? Thankfully I hear the trend is changing and expats are staying longer. I trust that I'll be one of them and that Farah and I will continue on the journey together for a while. I'm very grateful that I took notice of the moment and said hello.

I walk to the south side of the observation deck ands see the desert stretch out from downtown. Two things come to mind—the poem "Ozymandias" and the Tower of Babel. I think about the idea of "Ozymandias," that leaders and the empires they build fall into decline and about the boasts of Babel to "build a tower to the heavens" to find security and praise. I've heard similar language from the developers of Dubai as I read about how they worked to turn a fishing village into a major international city in just a few decades time. I turn to my right and walk over to see Dubai Marina and all its skyscrapers clustered in the distance. While they are true architectural achievements and works of art, they're ultimately just empty structures. They can't provide lasting security or eternal fame. But the souls of people living and working in them, those matter in the long-term.

The Emiratis, who are Muslims, have everything they need, except the one thing that matters: Jesus. The only thing I can bring them, the only thing we can bring them is the presence of Jesus. The city stands tall, shiny, and modern amidst "the lone and level sands that stretch far away," and the Burj Khalifa (aka the Vertical City) reaches into the heavens to make a name for the people. Dubai was built for the world to visit and invest in; it was built so it wouldn't be lost among its oil-rich neighbors in the years to come. But God only cares about their hearts, not their buildings. He sees them without their brilliantly tall tower, and He loves them.

EXTRAVAGANT DAILY TIME WITH JESUS
GEORGE BEST

The when, where, how, what and why of abiding for me are:

When: When I hit middle age, I contracted what my father called "old man disease"—waking up at 4:30 a.m. I'm not sure if it's age or the stress and responsibility that come with age, but pretty much every single day, I can't sleep past 5 a.m. I have embraced it rather than tried to fight it. So, early in the morning, I feed upon the Word of God and call upon His name.

Where: Generally the first part of my abiding time takes place in my bedroom. My wife heads to her little office, and I have the room and desk to myself. The second hour is my prayer time, and location varies depending on the day.

How and what: I start my first hour reading the Word. I don't journal, but every year I buy a sweet Moleskin notebook with grand intentions for the year ahead. Instead, technology and the wonderful little Tecarta Bible app give me a way to jot down my thoughts and the Spirit's leadings as I study. The app allows me to highlight with different colors, add notes beside verses, and create folders to place verses that speak to me. I'm a minimalist, so I love the fact that it's small and tidy and goes wherever I go.

My Bible of choice is the 1984 NIV, though I often find myself reading in the NLT as well, as it resonates with my simple spirit. I first read Psalms as it puts my heart in a right attitude. I then read a chapter in the Old Testament and the New Testament and the Gospels. Since dedicating my life to Jesus,

I love to read the Gospels every day no matter the time of year. After my scripture reading, I usually read from Oswald Chamber's *My Utmost For His Highest*, a family tradition passed down to us from my grandmother.

My prayer hour varies each day. My buddy Luke prays with me twice every week at 6 a.m. These are great prayer times as we encourage each other to press in and fight for faith. Some mornings I jump in the car and drive around the city. It takes me one hour to circle the city in prayer. I love this—it helps me stay focused. Other mornings I put on my winter cap and circle the medina of my city (the old Arabic/walled town). It takes me one hour to prayer walk that route. Some mornings I curl up next to my wife, and we spend one-half hour praying together for the things on our hearts. Other mornings I put music on and march around calling up the name of the Lord, shouting out and dancing before Him. I have a strong case of ADHD, and if I try to sit still and pray, my mind starts to wander. The next thing I know, I'm lost in la-la land.

At 7:15, my kids and wife join me for 30 minutes. Some mornings I strum on the guitar and we sings songs from the 1980s. Other mornings, my gifted son shreds on his Fender and we sing Hillsong, Chris Tomlin and other names I know nothing about. We then pray for a different subject each day and work on a memory verse together. The clock hits 7:45, and we're out the door for the school, etc.

Why: As each year of life goes by, I realize more and more how weak and helpless I am. Most mornings, I wake up with a tremendous weight and oppression on my chest. If I did not spend time in the presence of Jesus and if I was not filled by the Spirit of God each day, I don't know if I would want to get out of bed—let alone wage war against the kingdom of darkness where we live.

After walking intimately with Jesus for the last 22 years, my first reaction and habit is to cry out to God with the first thoughts of the morning, "Oh Lord, I am desperate for you today. I need you." This past year 2 Corinthians 12:9 has been my anchor verse: "'My grace is sufficient for you, for my power is made perfect in weakness.' Therefore, I will boast all the more gladly about my weaknesses, so that Christ's power may rest on me." What joy fills my soul as I cling to this promise! It gives me hope, not only in ministry, but also as a husband, father, and friend.

LIVING LIFE TO THE FULL
ARLENE WHITE

E veryone is bound to the patterns of this world. God wants us to be transformed from a sinful, destructive pattern to the harmonious, loving, and just pattern of His Kingdom. Only Jesus can break the sin pattern and truly transform people through renewing their minds. And everyone needs the renewal and transformation Jesus gives, each one of us, young and old, rich and poor, Arab and American, Christian and Muslim.

Jesus used stories and word pictures to teach His disciples the mysteries of the Kingdom of God. But our words alone cannot give justice to the things that God alone can do, which is especially the case with the value of transformation. To put into words what God is doing in our lives and in the lives of others would keep us at our computers day and night, typing as long as we live.

So, to give just a glimpse of what transformation looks like in us and in those to whom we minister, I offer some word pictures and some life stories that will hopefully open hearts even more to the infinite possibilities of God's transforming power.

THE ONION EFFECT

I often have many questions when it comes to transformation: Can Muslims be transformed? What can I do to be a part of transformation in a Muslim's life? When does faith begin? Is transformation instantaneous or gradual? How will I know if someone is being impacted by the gospel?

I used to think that conversion was a singular moment in time, a moment when the truth of Jesus and his death and his gift of salvation was revealed in someone's mind and that person mentally reached out and took the gift. While this might have been true in some sense for me, my Muslim friends have a very different background. They are a bit more like onions with many layers. I see the layers peel back, and each layer peeled back is both a real victory and a necessary step of faith for them to come to a full understanding of the gospel and to make a commitment to be a follower of Christ. As for which peeled back layer of that onion represents "the beginning of faith" or "conversion" or "salvation," I cannot pretend to know. I just believe this whole process of peeling back the layers of the onion is called transformation.

Our friend Seif runs a local restaurant. He quickly came to our aid in helping us navigate the city and learn cultural things. He also made himself available as a friend, and he and my husband have spent hours and hours together over the years. Though he was very hard and cynical to the gospel message at first, over time we have seen the layers of the onion peel back. He is now exploring the Bible and researching Christianity, and is always open to discuss and learn more with my husband.

Sahar is an employee in our business. A mother of two small boys, she was delighted to receive a part-time job that gives her work experience, gets her out of the house, and gives her social interaction with adults. We've had many opportunities to share the gospel with her, and yet just as impacting has been her witnessing our work ethic and integrity in business matters. She is taking steps of discovery, asking spiritual questions and grappling with the answers. While she has not made a distinct conversion, she is clearly being transformed by the impact of godly living and the gospel in her life. Those layers of the onion are peeling back. At a work party, she told me, "I'm not the same person you hired a year ago." I agree and am thankful, trusting God with the continual transformation He is working in her life.

Erin is a single woman on our team. She has walked with Jesus for a long time, but I'm amazed and blessed at the transformation I see happening in her life. She arrived here with insecurities and fears (as we all do). She is learning to trust her teammates and open up about her fears, believing God wants to use her weakness to bring glory to himself. The layers are peeling back, and the gospel is transforming both Erin and others through her. She is learning to lean on Christ for everything. She has many relationships with local women that through humility and transparency, God is using her to pass on a message of restoration and wholeness.

THE SEED EFFECT

Our family has been living and laboring in the Arab world for five years. During this time we have spent hours learning language, starting and working at our business, meeting new people daily, and praying regularly for transformation in the lives of those with whom we interact. It has been a season of plowing and sowing seeds in our community—every prayer, a seed; every attempt to learn and speak Arabic, a seed; and every conversation and act of love, a seed. Every time we've prayed for people's needs in Jesus' name has been a seed. Each time we've sat over coffee in a local coffee shop has been with every intention of planting seeds. The business was started to meet the felt needs in the community and was done so in an effort to plant seeds in people's lives.

Take Yousra, a cashier at my local grocery store. As I check out, I greet her by name, ask how she's doing, and let her know that I pray for her. She knows I am a Christian and I pray to Jesus. She shares things with me that she wants prayer for and lets me know how God has answered in her life. I believe and pray that God will reveal himself to her and that I will be available to explain more to her when that happens.

Aymen is a young man who spends a lot of time with our college interns. He has enjoyed hours of conversation, helping them with Arabic, and showing them around. He agreed to study the Word with my husband and a friend and seemed to have great insight into what he was reading, but after some time he stopped studying. We continued to spend time with him and after a year he showed interest again. It was during this further study that he made a decision to live as a Christian and be baptized. He expresses his journey as a "love story" of God pursuing him. He continues to slowly grow in his faith, understanding, and obedience.

THREE ENCOUNTERS

When we talk about transformation here, we often say that for a Muslim to come to Jesus, to experience transformation, it takes an interweaving of three encounters—a love encounter, a truth encounter, and a power encounter. A love encounter is a physical act, life on life, like attending weddings, making hospital visits, and meeting felt needs of a person or community. A truth encounter is a verbal presentation of the gospel, a Bible study, and a call to repentance. A power encounter is supernatural intervention—a miracle, healing, or an obvious answer to prayer. We encourage team members to do one act of love, one communication of truth, and one prayer in faith for the miraculous each day.

The Bible is pretty clear that faith comes by hearing, so we do place a priority on verbal proclamation of the gospel. We believe it's necessary and biblical to serve those that we proclaim to with loving deeds.

My onion and seed stories offer just a glimpse of what transformation looks like in the Arab world, but you can see this same kind of work of transformation happen wherever you are, every day. The more we can grasp the importance of each onion layer peeled back and of each seed sown, the more we can pray and serve with joy, fully anticipating that God will work the transformation, that He will empower the seed sowing, and that He will do the hard work of peeling back layers to bring forth a harvest.

PRAYER FOR UNREACHED PEOPLES

Arab, Gulf of United Arab Emirates
(2,050,000; 0.3% EVANGELICAL)

Pray that believers among the Gulf Arabs would proclaim the message of the gospel clearly, making the most of every opportunity God places before them (Col. 4:2–5).

STOP TEN

A Walk Through Muscat

Muscat is the ancient capital of the Sultanate of Oman whose empire once reached from Zanzibar to India. Its position at the southeastern end of the Arabian Peninsula made its port an important trading hub between the Arabian Gulf, the Indian subcontinent, and Asia. The city's remote location, situated at the farthest point of the Arab world, and the country's lack of major political unrest often keep it and its unreached Omani Arab Muslims from the public eye.

A WALK THROUGH MUSCAT

I t's early. I wake up with the call to prayer. Like every day. My husband and I get out of bed and join with our own prayers at home. We get the children up, and after breakfast it's time for school. I'm in language school most mornings while my kids are homeschooled, and we all each lunch together. The city comes to a halt in the afternoons. Businesses close, and people nap or enjoy family time until activity kicks back in around five o'clock. I then put on my black abaya, kandora, pants, and headscarf and venture out to visit my neighbors, accompanied by my children or my husband. My visit lasts about an hour before we walk home and have dinner. We put the kids to bed, sleep, and repeat.

This is life in hot, dusty Muscat, a city that seems more like a village than Oman's largest city and capital, which it is. It's only been in the last decade that roads were paved. There are no skyscrapers, but there is plenty of traffic with crazy drivers. With no trees, all there is to see is desert and rocky mountains situated along the Gulf of Oman. And it's hot, typically around 120 degrees.

Each day might look much the same for me, but that is not to say that life is ever tedious or boring. In fact, I find life here fascinating. My own neighborhood is a great example. Our street is sand; there is no pavement. Each time we drive on it, we make our own road as we go. Their houses are mud brick and much smaller than what we know in America, yet there could be as many as twenty-plus people living in these multigenerational households. The Omani people have servants, mostly from Pakistan, India and Afghanistan. We also have Balushi people in our neighborhood. This people group from Pakistani and Iran has lived in Oman for hundreds of years but is considered a lower class by the Omani people. My Omani friends find it strange when I visit a Balushi friend or shake a servant's hand.

This whole thing has been a learning process, especially in my visits with my neighbors. Life is strict for my friends here, and my friends are women only. First and foremost, it is modestly at all costs. It is required to wear the abaya, kandora (a floor-length dress), pants, and headscarf. I got in trouble once for not wearing pants under my kandora; the ladies checked.

Many friends wear their headscarves in their home as well. A young man my husband met said that he has never seen his mother's face or hair. It is risky for a woman to show her ankles, wrists, or a wisp of hair. Doing so could ruin her reputation, and her reputation is everything.

The lives of my friends have revolved around finding and keeping a husband. Most of them were married as teenagers, and they now have ten to twelve children. As they aim to keep and please their husbands, beauty is very important to them. They will take any chance to visit the salon, even though only their husbands will see their hair. They are also very religious. They carry counters in their hands to track how many times they say "God." They believe any time they say "praise God," they get points.

I know life sounds stringent for my friends, but the women are very sweet to me. Let me describe my time with them. It is about five o'clock, so I start preparing for my daily visit down the street. I pull out my abaya, kandora, pants, and headscarf, and get dressed. About 5:30, my boys accompany me on the short walk down the sand road to our neighbors. We pass some boys rough-housing in the street and some workers who just stare at me as we pass. This is all very normal to me now. I practice my Arabic and my greetings as we go, and I say a prayer for my visit as I arrive at my friend's house and ring the doorbell. We are ushered into the women's receiving room; there are, of course, no men around.

Women mostly stay in their houses. Their lives are spent entertaining guests, so visits are very formal. I shake my friend's hand and kiss her three times on the cheek and say my greetings. We will keep offering greetings until she stops. As I take a seat, she serves fruits, dates, and coffee. The topic of conversation inevitably turns to children, and I will be asked again if I will have any more. I've gotten used to this question, too. I smile and say "no." When the visit is over, my friend will bring out bakhoor, or incense. She places it under my dress as part of the tradition to smell nice for our husbands. Upon leaving, I share blessings in Arabic: "May God protect you. May God give you long life. May God be gracious to you." This connects with my friend counting mentions of God. My boys walk me home to the end of another day.

Sure, many days might look the same, but opportunities for friendship are not lacking. I have one friend who is in her thirties and, according to tradition, now past the age of marriage. Typically, when a woman turns thirty-two, she is considered "unmarriable" and will live with her parents until they pass, at which point she will live with her brother. But my friend had a different plan placed before her—her parents intended to send her as an Islamic missionary to a country in the West. I drove her to her interview for the assignment and talked her out of it. She is the most religious member of her family and always seeking God. In the past year, she has seen visions of Jesus and has asked to do a Bible study. What lies ahead of her? I am not sure, but I look forward to finding out. It is just such glorious opportunities like this that break up any monotony that we might feel here.

EXTRAVAGANT DAILY TIME WITH JESUS
JEFF GRIFFIN

M y daily time with Jesus involves about an hour and a half of Bible study and prayer over a cup of coffee at the start of each day. Well, actually two cups!

BIBLE STUDY

I have trouble just reading the Bible—I tend to fall asleep. So most of my Bible study involves copying out Scriptures, a habit I was taught the day after I surrendered my life to Christ, during my first year at university. A former student who was back on a visit took me under his wing and taught me how to use a concordance and look up verses on a particular topics and to copy them out by hand in a notebook. Later, I was taught how to do a sentence flow chart to understand the thought flow of a passage and how to study whole books. But the practice of writing out Scriptures has stayed with me to this day. It enables me to meditate on the verses in a way that reading does not, and draw out the trust from God's Word.

Occasionally, I will read through the whole Bible using a one-year Bible. This helps me understand Scriptures in their context. Most recently I did this with a one-year Bible arranged chronologically.

To help me draw out the lessons from a passage, I now look for the following. Is there:

- A command for me to obey?
- A promise for me to claim?
- A sin for me to avoid or repent of?
- An example for me to follow (good) or avoid (bad)?
- A truth to believe?
- A prayer to pray?

More recently, for our work with chronological Bible storytelling, we have come across a set of questions that I find useful to study a story: What do we learn about God/Jesus in this story? What do we learn about man? How can we apply this in our lives?

PRAYER

For my prayer time, I like to walk around praying aloud, again to help me stay focused and alert, not falling asleep.

For the first part of my prayer time, I do two things. First, I surrender myself to God, verbally bringing my life as a daily offering to God, and offering myself as a living sacrifice holy and acceptable to God, which is our true spiritual worship (Romans 12:1–2). Another verse I might repeat in doing this is: "Your kingdom come, your will be done in my life as in heaven" (from the Lord's Prayer) and "Not my will, but yours be done" (Luke 22:42).

Second, I pray aloud to take up the full armor of God, listing each item and verses from God's Word that speak about that part of the armor. I found this necessary to keep on top of my emotions. I name each part of the armor and verses associated with each, personalizing them, for example, with the shield of faith: "The just shall live by faith" (Romans 1:17 NJKV); "We live by faith not by sight" (2 Corinthians 5:7); "Faith is the substance of things hoped for, the evidence of things not seen" (Hebrews 11:1 NKJV); I trust in you with all my heart, I lean not on my own understanding, I acknowledge you in all my ways, and trust that you will direct my paths (Proverbs 3:5–6).

Sometimes for variety I will pray the Lord's Prayer, expanding and personalizing each line. It covers the same areas plus others. Or another prayer I pray, usually for coworkers but also for myself, is Paul's prayer for the Colossians (1:9–12).

Then I have an intercession time with a different focus each day: coworkers, team members, the lost, authorities, national believers, and the church.

Two last things about abiding: I have never been very successful at Scripture memorization. I tried this early on in my Christian walk, but never really picked it up as a habit. But I have found that two habits I have incorporated enable me to memorize Scripture without directly trying. First, the habit of copying Scriptures indents significant verses in my memory. Second, praying Scriptures and quoting them in my prayers regularly does the same thing. The objective is different—to use the Scriptures in praying—but the result is the same: Scripture memorization.

Last, God revolutionized my devotional time in 1998 when, along with a challenge to begin fasting and praying for our area, He asked me to give up my Saturday take-it-easy morning. Until that time, I prayed and read my Bible each day, but Saturday was always a day I left for sleeping in a little. I would read my Bible quickly and skip prayer. God put His finger on that and said: "I want you to give me every day, including Saturday." That transformed my devotional time with Jesus. I became far more disciplined.

"Faith is the substance of things hoped for, the evidence of things not seen"

— HEBREWS 11:1

SERVE TOGETHER IN HUMILITY
JEFF GRIFFIN

W hy do we choose partnership over independence? It's simple. We can't do it alone. There are so many who are unreached and so few trying to reach them. We need to work together to accomplish this enormous task. This means partnering with other believers.

Partnership occurs on many levels. We partner with God. We put aside our personal preferences to partner with our own coworkers, and we display humility and an appreciation for the greater body of Christ when we partner with other nationalities, agencies and organizations, and multiple generations. Partnership describes our relationship with the local indigenous church when we partner with them to reach their own people.

PARTNER WITH GOD

When my wife and I moved to the interior of North Africa to work among farmers, we struggled to find our bearings in our first year. While at a conference, we prayed, "Jesus, show us Your strategy for how to plant Your church in this place." The answer came loud and clear: fast and pray. So we began fasting one day each week and going on three-day fasts every few months.

In April, I invited some local believers from the capital city to visit and follow up on Bible-correspondence-course contacts in our city. I had tried to do this previously but found that it was too high profile and dangerous for me as an expat in our area. In their first visit, they connected with four contacts that said they were believers. They came back every few months, and each time they located new believers. It was out of these contacts that the first church was birthed. By the end of the year, we could look back and see how much God had done, all because we started to fast and pray.

CONNECT WITH COWORKERS

The most successful team I have been part of never deliberately set out to be a team. We came together around a new church that a coworker had planted and were together for about three years. There were five of us involved: the coworker who started the group with a local believer and a Latino coworker, an older couple with great Arabic and years of wisdom and experience, and me.

I was reluctant to get involved initially for fear of expats outnumbering local believers. But I saw there was a need to develop the worship, and since I played the guitar I got involved and spent the next two years developing this part of the group: putting together a songbook, providing the music, leading worship, and teaching one of the believers to play the guitar.

This illustrates the best of partnership because we all worked together for a specific, common goal—planting a church—and each took different roles and responsibilities, developed those, and then intentionally handed them over to the local believers. We intentionally worked on training believers to take over, and we all exited one by one. The older couple was the last to leave, after about three and a half years.

JOIN WITH LOCALS

Partnering with locals is a simple step we can easily overlook. We can come to the field so full of vision and passion that we drive a new church plant. Part of the art of church planting is to impart vision to believers so that they lead the church plant, not us. When this happens we run with them and it takes off.

The coworker who birthed the church in the capital city told me once that he followed up several Bible-correspondence-course contacts until he found one that had no ulterior motives and whom he felt he could trust. Then he began to work with him, imparting a vision for the church. They partnered together to start the church. This believer eventually took over as pastor and to this day is one of the key national believers in his nation.

TELL THE STORY

During our time in North Africa, we developed a close relationship with one particular family. We had begun to work on a project to develop a set of Bible stories to share God's plan of salvation with Muslims. We then began to visit this family each month to share these stories with them, partly to test them out, partly to proclaim the gospel to them. The children loved the stories, and we learned later that the oldest daughter began to believe during this time.

Later, a coworker visited this family with a local believing friend named Abel. Abel had helped us translate the stories into the local dialect. Our coworker realized that the family already knew a lot, and he challenged the family to follow Christ. The father had allowed us to reach his children but had held back himself. However, when he saw Abel, a local citizen like himself, he got excited and accepted the Lord. Later he and the whole family were baptized. I can remember the incredible smile of joy on his face after his baptism.

We partnered with Abel to produce the stories. We labored for hours on the original stories and drank many glasses of sweet mint tea with this local family as we shared the gospel. Finally, Abel and a coworker visited the family and led them to Christ.

These Bible stories continued to be used today as local believers continue to plant the church in indigenous soil.

PRAYER FOR UNREACHED PEOPLES

Arab, Omani of Oman

(1,036,000; 1.2% EVANGELICAL)

Pray that the Omani Arabs will understand that hope for forgiveness and acceptance with God is available only through Jesus' work on the cross (1 Cor. 1:18).

STOP ELEVEN

A Walk Through Sana'a

Sana'a, the capital of Yemen, is part of biblical Sheba, which spanned modern-day Yemen and Ethiopia. Sana'a has been inhabited for more than 2,500 years and in the 7th and 8th centuries it was a major center for the propagation of Islam. Thirteen centuries later, nearly 100 percent of the Yemeni people are still Muslim. This city and state that once flourished along ancient trade routes now languishes amidst political crisis brought about by the protests of the Arab Spring.

A WALK THROUGH SANA'A

I heard a story on this morning's news of a Yemeni mother and her daughters returning home only to be held at the border. Without her husband, the woman and her family could not make the necessary trip through Saudi Arabia; they needed a male escort. American passports in hand, they were ready to fly home to Dearborn, Michigan, but their husband and father was not traveling with them because he had not yet received his citizenship.

I'm not sure I can fully imagine their plight, though I know something about the current situation in Yemen. It's dark and difficult. The country faces famine, and the fighting continues. I talk to my Yemeni friends on a daily or weekly basis by text message or by phone call and I know things are dire. But I have hope.

About a year before the Arab Spring, a number of other missionary families in the country felt God calling them out. We and a several other missionaries continued to pray and felt that God told us to stay. The Holy Spirit also spoke a word that Yemen faced a huge shaking followed by a huge outpouring. We had no idea what was coming. We stayed through the Arab Spring, about two more years, but then God saw fit to have us leave. We now watch from a distance at the shaking Yemen endures today and still believe that after the shaking will come the outpouring.

The outpouring is coming to the shop owner Mohammed in the old city of Sana'a. I met him in the mid-1990s when I first moved to Yemen. I remember he had such a great eye for old silver. He bought old silver pieces and beads to make jewelry, and he would let my friend and I into the back room to sift through bowls and bowls of these pieces to make our own. He was so fascinating; he loved his culture and knew the history. Yemen once had a very large Jewish population; they were amazing silversmiths and made jewelry. He could look at a silver piece and tell which one of the three main Jewish families of old Sana'a it came from and the approximate time it was made. We shared the gospel with him and gave him an Arabic Bible. Seeds for an outpouring were planted.

Throughout the rest of the old city of Sana'a with its original walls and gates and 3,000-year-old cobblestone streets, the outpouring will happen. I often took visitors to the old city to see the tourist section and the many wares of Yemen for sale like the *jambeya*, the traditional large curved knife Yemeni men wear at their waists. We walked to the Yemeni food court with its not-very-clean restaurants and their rusted, rundown tables. The food was delicious though, and the temperature was always hot enough to kill anything suspect. While many smells in the city were not pleasant, the food court smelled wonderful because of the special Yemeni bread, the kebabs and a Yemeni version of *fuul* (beans) with jalapenos, tomato, onion and garlic. Throughout the old city our eyes were filled with the geometric patterns on all the houses, which looked much gingerbread. The houses were designed for animals to live on the ground floor and the family on the floors above. Animals on the ground floor were very common in the villages, but this only happened in the old city of Sana'a, not the newer section of the capital. I think back to those houses and their families now, and I pray for the outpouring to rush in.

I fondly remember one busy intersection in the city. There was no traffic light, only a traffic cop in the center. To many newcomers it looked like chaos. There is no such thing as a straight line or lane in Yemen. Everyone inches forward and two lanes become four to see who can reach the front first. On one side of the intersection were a wedding hall and the busiest restaurant in the city. The louder it was, the better the wedding. As women gathered for wedding festivities, the men waited in the cars or milled around the street. I think about those crowds of people celebrating and look forward to the outpouring reaching them.

The Yemeni are such kind, warm, hospitable, generous people. Wherever we went, they always invited us into their homes and generously shared their history and their tea. Often Americans hear "Yemen" and associate the country with Al Qaeda and Osama bin Laden or the bombing of the U.S.S. Cole. One would think by watching the news that my Yemeni friends must all be dangerous. These are the people that when we asked for directions, they dropped everything and took us to the place. No matter the cause any of us fight for, I still care about them and they about me. I trust the outpouring is for those on both sides of the fighting.

Yemen is so different from the West and even from the Arab countries that surround it. There was a Pizza Hut but it was nothing like Pizza Hut in America. The Baskin Robbins is more like home, though. Beyond that,

Yemen has no Western style restaurants or chains, and the men, only half of them in Sana'a wear Western clothing. The poorest country in the Arab world, unlike any of its neighbors, unique in most every way, suffers terribly. But I remember God's Word, and I believe that outpouring is coming.

Hundreds of missionaries lived in Yemen and planted many seeds through the years. Proclamation of the gospel happened. Yemenis have very good memories, especially for oral stories, and the gospel stories will take root. Bibles upon Bibles were passed out over the years, like the one to my shopkeeper friend. While many workers have gone, the Bibles remain. I believe these seeds are about to sprout and take root. It's time.

EXTRAVAGANT DAILY TIME WITH JESUS
MARY SCOTT

When my alarm first sounds at 5:00 a.m., I admit I am less than enthused. I always considered myself a "night person." The glorious handful of hours after our kids went to sleep were pure gold! I would sink comfortably into the couch and enjoy the next captivating episode in the latest Netflix series, my hands wrapped around a warm mug of tea. Ultimate rest, I thought.

When I was introduced to the idea of a time tithe to the Lord, I scoffed a bit. Honestly, who had time for that? But I felt a nudge inside me. So I considered the possibility of setting aside large portions of my time to focus on my relationship with God, to re-center on Him, to abide in Jesus fully. I began slowly—fifteen minutes here and there throughout the day. I experimented with times in the late mornings, evenings, and afternoons before finally realizing that my mind is most clear and most open in the wee hours before dawn. I discovered I best and fully connect with the Creator of the universe after a restful night's sleep. There in the still quiet of the morning, before our two small children wake up, I invite the Spirit of God to come into my day and speak to my soul.

In the dim light of our living room, I open a devotional and allow the words to seep in. I imagine it's like the flowers opening to the sun in the morning. Those first words of challenge or encouragement awaken my heart to His purposes. A few minutes of spoken worship are followed by a time of praying through a list of requests I keep tucked in a journal. I spend a large portion of my time consuming the Scriptures. Later in the day, between studying Arabic, meeting with our team, and ministering to friends and neighbors, I find moments to read and study the thoughts and perspectives of my favorite authors and theologians.

Of course, I'd like to say my time spent with the Lord in the mornings always runs smoothly—that I jump out of bed with the same enthusiasm each and every day, that our little ones never wake early and distract my reading. But that is certainly not the case. When it comes down to it, spending undivided time abiding in Christ is truly a discipline. It's a muscle that requires strengthening. I can say, if we don't value and prioritize our time with Him, we can be certain it will fall to the outer folds of our minds and our lives.

As a parent of three small children and a full-time student of Arabic who also teaches English and participates in team life in a culture not my own, some might wonder how I can afford to spend this excessive amount of time with the Lord. I would challenge that notion—I can't afford not to. I cannot minister to and comfort my abused neighbor; I cannot share the gospel with my English students; I cannot pray with our Bedouin friend battling cancer; and I cannot walk these streets swarming with the lost without being rooted in the strength and power of the Spirit of God. I simply don't have inside me what I need to achieve even the smallest bit of what He calls me to. I must abide in Him.

PAY WHATEVER PRICE
STEPHEN AND MARY SCOTT

We recently traveled outside the city to a neighboring village to help a local pastor and his wife with an outreach they do with refugees living nearby. They bring the kids out by bus once or twice a week for a small program and a light meal. This week our son Eric was a super helper. He led songs, helped with a game, and passed out sandwiches; he had such excitement about helping out at the event. We pray that Jesus continues to cultivate that excitement in his heart. But it's a prayer that leaves us with a lump in our throats because we know what challenges we face as a family in our next home.

THE COST OF SACRIFICE

There's something romantic about pioneer missions—the thought of packing up select belongings and hurling oneself into another culture, language, and way of life. When we first moved to the Middle East a decade ago, our romantic ideal meter was through the roof.

Over time though, it's been both a challenge and a balancing act to remove the romance but keep the heart. Refining and sharpening has taken place, with sacrifice becoming the most brutal of honors. It's come in degrees. First it was the sacrifice of the comforts of our home culture: restaurants, clean parks, and libraries. Then we had children and the degree of sacrifice cut deeper— grandparents farther away, schools not as fit, activities not as abundant.

Our Live Dead value statement for sacrifice says, "We commit ourselves to pay whatever price is necessary." We can see that Jesus has been expanding our capacity for sacrifice, preparing us to pay whatever price, even as we face our most immense challenge yet: Will we go and plant the church in a country known for violence? Will we subject our family to a culture that has been steeped in war for years? Could we send our children to the best possible school, one that is still not up to our public school standards in the States and one in which our children will most likely be bullied simply for being foreigners?

God met us with an answer through a believer we met during a visit. When we asked about schools, he responded very candidly: "The children here are very aggressive, but trust that your children are the Lord's and He will take care of them. It's not up to you." Those words hit hard. We would never knowingly put my children in harm's way, but we're realizing there is an element of sacrifice that Jesus wants to teach them as well.

God is not just calling us as husband and wife. He's beckoning our children into this new place to share the gospel as well. He is drawing our entire family into His Kingdom work in a difficult place. Our children will make disciples, too. We see Eric's excited face singing songs and handing out sandwiches, and we have to trust that Jesus will cultivate that heart in our new home as well. There is a price. It will cost us something. But it's also our call.

THE PERSPECTIVE OF SACRIFICE

There's an interesting thing that happens to hearts that have the right perspective on sacrifice. They end up saying, "I never made a sacrifice." On December 4, 1857, David Livingstone, the great pioneer missionary, was telling Cambridge University students about his work in Africa. Someone asked him what it was like to leave the "benefits" of England. He answered, "People talk of the sacrifice I have made in spending so much of my life in Africa.… Away with the word in such a view, and with such a thought! It is emphatically no sacrifice. Say rather it is a privilege."[6]

As we look at the reality of what this new calling means for our family, the list of obstacles is long. First, living conditions. The land is hot and smelly, and most of the buildings are in disrepair. Second, utilities. Power is unreliable, salty water comes from the tap, and housing is expensive. Third, family. The schooling system is poor and very Islamic. We hope the school will be adequate for our three children, but we know we will have to supplement and guard them from false teachings. Finally, the political situation. It's daunting. In our previous homes, soldiers were the people you ran to, but in this new place soldiers are representatives of different militias. Whether that soldier helps or not is up to whose side that militia is on.

But for all the obstacles, there are opportunities. The church there is vibrant—breathtaking, really. The believers involved are convinced that conditions will worsen even while the opportunities to share increase. We see that they've been called to sacrifice, and we call it a privilege to join them.

Our friend there told us: "We have all eternity to enjoy stable governance in heaven. Why not put up with the instability on earth for a few decades?"

Moving to this deeply sensitive place is a difficult calling. It does include sacrifice. But pioneer church planting in the Arab world will nearly always include that. If it were easy, the church would already be planted. We prayed that the Lord would make our decision easy, that it would be obvious from the moment we set foot in the city that we were supposed to be here. Alas, we were too earthly minded in our first evaluation and thought, "How could we do this?" But thank God for second chances to evaluate! At first, we mistook the poor infrastructure we encountered as a release from God's call in our lives, but all praise to Jesus who calls us to difficult things!

We believe now that choosing not to pioneer because the calling is too difficult is choosing not to pioneer at all. Choosing to walk with Christ without suffering is choosing not to walk with Him at all. We thank Him for the privilege to go.

And we don't believe we're the only family being given offered this privilege. There are too few workers for this abundant harvest. We can't fathom that the Father has only called our family and a few others to reach these people. We believe He's asking more people to lay down their ambitions, their comforts, and maybe even their lives to pick up their crosses and drag them through the sands of the Arab world so the lost can hear.

Arab, Northern Yemeni of Yemen

(10,817,000; 0% EVANGELICAL)

The Bible tells us to pray for the peace of Jerusalem (Ps. 122:6) and to pray for all people (1 Tim. 2:1–4). Pray that the Northern Yemeni Arabs would experience peace not only in their nation but also in their hearts. Pray for the peace that results when men and women are reconciled with God (John 14:27). Pray for men and women of peace among the Northern Yemeni Arabs (Luke 10:6).

STOP TWELVE

A Walk Through Jeddah

The final stop on the journey is Jeddah, a modern commercial port city on the Red Sea with resort hotels, beaches, and seafront promenade featuring King Fahd's Fountain, the tallest water fountain in the world. The second largest city in Saudi Arabia, Jeddah is the gateway to the religious center of the Muslim world. Here Muslims from around the world begin their pilgrimages to the Islamic holy cities of Mecca and Medina.

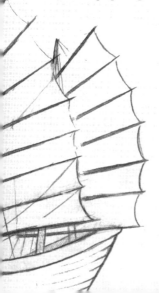

A WALK THROUGH JEDDAH

I pick up my tall mocha at the counter and turn to leave the local Starbucks. I walk out into the fading sunlight as a couple of guys on Harley Davidsons roll in. My husband and I walk across the parking lot and head for the walking path beside the water. I feel the wind blow off the water. It was another hot, humid day, making me grateful again for the sea breeze.

The whole area along the waterfront has filled up tonight. There are men running and women power-walking, kids flying kites, and families picnicking. We watch the last few jet skiers coming off the water and Filipino men fishing along the shore. We pass a little kid selling mint-flavored gum and trinkets and those glow stick things. He's hard to resist. We give him about six riyals for some gum and a glow-in-the-dark necklace. It's on nights like these that I feel a little homesick. I mean, seeing all the people, the picnics, the glow sticks – it's like Fourth of July here. Except it's not. This isn't Jacksonville; it's Jeddah. It's not America; it's Saudi Arabia. Life is so different here, but sometimes it feels familiar.

We continue our walk along the Corniche, the stretch of beaches and coves that runs the length of Jeddah along the Red Sea, breathing in both the smell of the sea and food cooking. We keep glancing at the horizon to make sure we don't miss the sunset. Earlier in the evening, families claimed their spots in the coves with their mats, and now they set out their picnics and coffee pots, and relax, enjoying various things like rotisserie chicken, French fries, salad, seasoned rice, and orange juice. This evening we skipped the picnic and went for burgers and fries from a nearby snack stand.

While the surroundings feel like any park in America, the people are quite an assortment. I see the women in abayas, including myself, but as the sun fades it is difficult to tell which wear the traditional black and which wear the newly fashionable blues and purples. Every woman has her head covered, though I don't notice any fully veiled faces tonight. There are as many men in traditional white thobes with red and white checked scarves as there are business suits and shorts and jeans and t-shirts. Come to think of it, even those guys back at the Starbucks riding the Harleys were wearing leather and Harley jackets.

We find a place to sit. My husband and I discovered that people are friendly but tend to keep to themselves unless we approach them. Tonight we sit down with our snacks and greet the family next to us. "Salam alaykum. Kayf halik?" ("Peace be upon you. How are you?") They seemed surprised and excited to hear us speak Arabic. They simply answer, "Al-humd-i-Allah" ("Praise God."). We meet many people around town, while running errands, just by saying hello and asking questions. Americans rarely speak Arabic or show knowledge of the culture, so whenever we do, immediately people want to connect. Often, after a few minutes we exchange phone numbers and make plans to meet for dinner, coffee or shopping trips. From there, friendships go deep fast.

In fact, I'm really looking forward to tomorrow evening. We're having dinner with a local Muslim family who also happens to be our biggest support system in this city. I get a bit overwhelmed when I think about them. If it weren't for this family, it would have been difficult to stay here early on. They helped us work through the issues of getting settled into our new place when we arrived, showing us such kindness, hospitality and acceptance. It is amazing how they have made us feel like family.

Muslim identity and family are everything to these people. Most of the extended family lives nearby, and they see each other regularly throughout the week at one or more family dinners. And while that seems different from my family back home, where we only see each other once or twice a year for holidays, the relationships between siblings and parents and grandparents are so much like my own. They love and care for each other. They argue and fight but always make up, and they watch out for one another. When I am with our Muslim friends, I feel like I am watching my own family.

I look around at all the people hanging out along the Corniche tonight, and I can't help but smile. Because people are people, no matter where you are in the world. I think about the ladies I've met here – each with personalities, dreams and hobbies that remind me of family and friends back home.

Breaking into our peaceful picnic is the screech of tires along the thoroughfare. "Kids these days," my husband smiles. And he's right, though maybe he shouldn't be laughing. Somewhere down the street now is a car of young guys pulling stunts. All that screeching of tires is a favorite pastime, aka drifting, or the art of acceleration before slamming on the brakes. It can be fascinating to watch but pretty dangerous and frowned upon by government.

But that doesn't always stop the bored, the daring, and the young from trying whatever crazy thing comes to their head.

This country is very young. The median age is around 26. Think of it: half the population is under 26 years old. With such a young population comes modernization. These young people remind me of young Americans. They are into mobile phones, Facebook, Twitter, YouTube, video games, you name it. They are engaged in the world around them, and they are a diverse group, difficult to generalize – some are fanatical, others more open-minded, with various levels of education and connection to urban culture.

Starbucks, Harleys, families picnicking, the youth, they all make Jeddah look very much like the West at times, but it's also a place that I never feel fully settled. I think my husband and I realize we don't have forever; each day is a little bit like borrowed time. Any day we could be kindly asked to leave. That reality can make pleasant nights like this on the Corniche very sobering. I sip my mocha, we eat our burgers, and looking around I see a lot of people that don't know Christ. I think of our Muslim friends, our family here, and other faces that we don't yet know, and I pray that God gives us connections tonight, tomorrow, tomorrow night, for as long as He will, and that we won't pass up any opportunity to say, "Salam alaykum."

EXTRAVAGANT DAILY TIME WITH JESUS
JON HODGES

I try to spend a regular time each morning and each evening in uninterrupted fellowship with Jesus. I will be the first to tell you that I do not always keep that uninterrupted time perfectly, yet it is one of the basic needs in my life and thus a priority that I strive for daily. When I am walking with Jesus daily, I am able to weather difficult storms that come my way, I am able to see God sovereign over my circumstances, and the core of my character and passions of my heart feel centered. Continual fellowship with Jesus renews my spirit and revives my soul.

My uninterrupted time with the Lord, my "quiet time," usually consists of some worship on the guitar, some Scripture reading, some listening, and some walking around the living room and speaking my heart to the Lord. It is rarely exactly the same; however, study of the Word and listening to the Lord speak are both core components of my quiet times.

MEDITATING ON THE WORD

Joshua 1:8 (NLT) counsels us: "Study this Book of Instruction continually. Meditate on it day and night so you will be sure to obey everything written in it. Only then will you prosper and succeed in all you do."

How do you study the Word? What does it mean to meditate on it versus to just read it? Do you have a plan to help you meditate on the Bible daily and nightly? Write a simple plan of Bible meditation for the week. Make note of which chapters you will read, how you will meditate on what you read, and how you might continue this meditation after this week.

LISTENING TO THE LORD

Jesus instructs us: "When you pray, don't babble on and on as people of other religions do. They think their prayers are answered merely by repeating their words again and again. Don't be like them, for your Father knows exactly what you need even before you ask him!" (Matthew 6:7–8 NLT).

How much do you listen and how much do you speak during your quiet times? Do you need to do more listening to the Lord or more speaking with the Lord? Do you ever journal what the Lord is speaking to you?

List some ways that you can actively listen to the Lord this week. How will you listen to the Lord? What will you do when He speaks to you? Will you write it down, will you record it, will you draw a picture representing it? How will you try to listen to the Lord throughout the day, not just during your quiet times?

WHO WE ARE DRIVES WHAT WE DO
JON HODGES

An old proverb says, "It's not about the destination; it's about the journey." This is certainly true regarding development of godly character. Our purpose is not to focus on our goal but to submit ourselves fully to the journey of refinement that the Lord sets us on. When we give ourselves over to the Lord's journey, without even realizing it, we will arrive at our destination and receive our reward.

The apostle Paul, in Romans 5:3, clearly charts our path. We see the first step of the journey is one of the scariest words in our dictionary, a word with so many dark and troubling connotations: *suffering*. "Not only so, but we also rejoice in our sufferings, because we know that suffering produces perseverance; perseverance, character; and character, hope. And hope does not disappoint us, because God has poured out his love into our hearts by the Holy Spirit, whom he has given us" (Romans 5:3–5). One of the key components to our journey toward character is suffering.

Paul instructs us in our attitude toward suffering: Rejoice in it! What a paradox, to rejoice in something that is by definition uncomfortable, frustrating, discouraging, and painful. One of the first things we need to do on our journey to godly character is to look at suffering as an opportunity, the gateway to the destination we are striving for.

But knowing that we should rejoice when suffering comes our way doesn't mean it will be enjoyable. We—and even the great heroes of the faith—rarely feel happy about suffering. However, the Bible doesn't teach us to be happy about it, but rather to rejoice in it.

The second and most crucial step in our journey toward character is perseverance. The trials, suffering, persecution—whatever you call them—will come. There is no question. Though it may look different and be of varying severity for each person, difficulty will confront you. The question then remains: What effect will those trials have on your character? Will they fortify the DNA of your soul? Much of this depends on whether you persevere.

Our response to and attitude in life's difficulties can reconstruct the DNA of our souls for the better or for the worse.

I remember one of our first earth-shattering trials on the field. My wife and I had arrived in one of the most gospel-resistant countries in the world, and we were ready for all types of demonic attack. We were ready to be shot at, targeted for kidnapping, spat upon, assaulted by manifest demons that would oppose God's work. We were ready! What we weren't prepared for was a painful and unexpected disagreement with a friend, believer, and colleague. We had thought we had prepared for it all, but here we were being attacked in the very area we had the least experience.

Those nights were agonizing, filled with frustration, anger, and bitterness. This trial brought out all shapes and forms of a monster living inside of me that I never knew resided there. The disagreement and my reaction to it shook the foundations of so many areas of my life that I had thought were solid. The poisons of bad attitude and hate began creeping up. I was ashamed of my response. This was the beautifully painful process of the reconstruction of my spiritual DNA. After months of dealing with the issue, I hit my fork in the road. My negative response up to that point had been a natural reaching reflecting the current state of my character. And the Lord and my friends began to challenge me to shift my attitude, to put down my flesh, and to persevere.

Little by little, I started to identify areas of my spirit and character that needed change. It was by the grace of God and through the help of the Holy Spirit that I was able to ask forgiveness where I was wrong and to intentionally begin to change my attitude.

About a year into this episode, the Lord gave me an epiphany that I will never forget. As I sat in my car, having just finished a phone call with the person with whom I had the conflict, the Lord dropped on me every area that I had been wrong in my spirit. Surprisingly, it was one of the most amazing feelings of freedom I have ever experienced. All I wanted to do was call all my close friends and tell them how the Lord had graciously broken me and corrected my arrogant and prideful attitude. A major piece of my character had been reconstructed, and I could not have felt better.

At the end of this journey through suffering and perseverance comes the building of our character. If you have opened your heart to the Lord's refinement during your trial, you will be changed. You will not only act more honestly, you will be more honest. People won't just perceive you as having integrity; you will be a man or woman of integrity. The more the Lord allows you to suffer under His powerful and precise hammer of refinement, the more you become a person of character.

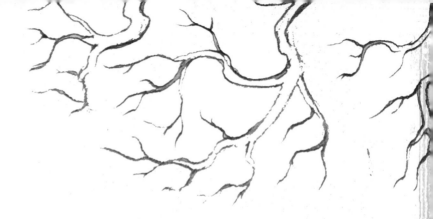

Arab, Saudi Najdi of Saudi Arabia

(12,041,000; 0.1% EVANGELICAL)

History tells us that the Church grows the most when persecution is present. Pray that the believers among the Saudi-Najdi Arabs will endure persecution in a Christ-like manner and will give their lives for the sake of the gospel if necessary (1 Peter 2:21–23).

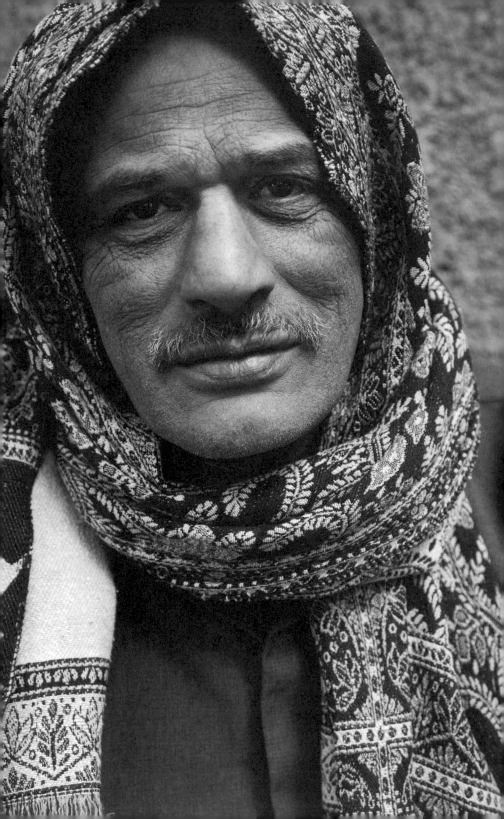

THE LIVE DEAD JOURNEY

you just experienced is an introduction to the values that undergird the Live Dead movement set in the context of the Arab world. The principles derived are applicable everywhere—as increasingly are the Arabs. Arabs are immigrating into North America, Europe, and other nations around the world. God is sending some of us to work among the Arabs and bringing some of the Arabs to our suburbs that we might work among them at home. It is our prayer that this Journey has moved your heart to see Arabs as God sees them, to break your heart that they may come to know Jesus.

live dead

HOW DOES LIVE DEAD WORK IN THE ARAB WORLD?

If your heart has been moved for Arab Muslims and you feel God might be calling you to live and die among precious unreached peoples in the Arab world, we would love to connect with you. If you are American and not affiliated with a mission organization, we ask that you apply to Assemblies of God World Missions at goag.org (Assemblies of God leads but does not own Live Dead; we intentionally want to cooperate with other likeminded agencies). If you are American and affiliated with a sending agency or a non-American, please have your agency leaders contact us at mobilization@ arabworld.livedead.org.

HOW YOU CAN GET INVOLVED IN LIVE DEAD ARAB WORLD

If *Live Dead Arab World The Journey* has given you a burden for the Arab world but you don't feel called to go, you are just as important to us and to Live Dead. You can help in several key ways:

1   INTERCESSION: Download the Live Dead prayer app (available for iOS and Android) and receive one unreached people group to pray for each day.

2   ADVOCACY: We are interested in mobilizing individuals and churches that will adopt one of our church-planting teams and help to raise up prayer, workers, and resources for those teams. More information can be found on the advocacy page of the website (livedead.org) or by emailing us at advocacy@livedead.org.

"The ultimate goal is to preach the gospel of the Kingdom among every people group on earth that Jesus might come back."

ENDNOTES

1   Todd M. Johnson and Gina A. Zurlo, "Ongoing Exodus: Tracking the Emigration of Christians from the Middle East," http://www.gordonconwell.edu/resources/documents/JMEPP-JohnsonaandZurlo.pdf.

2   Harold Sala, *Heroes: People Who Made a Difference in Our World* (Uhrichsville, OH: Barbour Publishing, 1998).

3   Ibid.

4   Heard from Dr. Alicia Britt Chole in a mentoring session in 2012. See www.leadershipii.com.

5   Adapted from *Practicing His Presence* by Brother Lawrence and Frank Laubach, SeedSowers Publishing, Jacksonville, FL.

6   Thanks to our friend Glenn Smith for sharing the Circles of Accountability with us. Find full details about the Three Circle Model from *Faithful and True* at www.faithfulandtrue.com.

7   Samuel Zwemer, "The Glory of the Impossible," in *Perspectives on the World Christian Movement*.

WHAT IS LIVE DEAD?

I n one sense, Live Dead is timeless and universal. It is the crucified life, the "I die daily" of Paul, the death to self that unbroken generations of Christ followers from all cultures have faithfully lived. All who bear the name of Jesus are called to put His passions and priorities above their own needs and comforts. We all are to live dead.

In another sense, Live Dead is a very intentional effort to preach the gospel of the Kingdom among every nation that the end may come (Matthew 24:14). Following the 1890s, the great century of Christian mission, came the realization that our world is not getting better, and that peace and justice cannot be ultimately realized by the efforts of man—including redeemed man. A longing, desperation for Christ to return, filled the hearts of believers in Jesus as the twentieth century dawned. Desperate for Jesus to come back, understanding that His return was linked to the gospel being preached to every people (to every ethno-linguistic group), aware that this could not be done in their own power, believers from around the world got on their knees and pleaded for power from on high.

One hundred years later we still pray, as William Carey suggested, with open Bible and open map, and see that there are yet 6,000-plus people groups who are unreached with the gospel. Forty percent of our world does not have a Christian friend.

Live Dead, in the specific sense then, is an effort to see Jesus glorified by every ethno-linguistic people on earth that the Scripture may be fulfilled and our King of Kings return to rule and reign forever. Jesus called us to make disciples of all peoples, and we are convinced that the best means to this is by planting churches. This is the nonnegotiable core of Live Dead: church planting among unreached peoples in teams.

The reality is that many of the peoples yet to be reached are found in contexts of oppression, war, restricted access, instability, poverty, and inhospitable climates. Some combination of manic ideology, spiritual oppression, political chaos, intemperate living conditions, unavailable schooling or health care, etc., makes these peoples very difficult to live among. If we are going to reach them (by planting churches among them, through teams), there is going to be a cost. It will not be easy. It will take blood and boldness, sacrifice and suffering, tears and tenacity. Some will be imprisoned, some will die, some will spend a lifetime of labor with little credit and little reward. All will have to live dead in one manner or another.

Missions in our era does not restrict the unreached to the rural poor. While it is true that many Muslim unreached people groups live in hard-to-reach and inhospitable places like Yemen and Libya, some of the most unreached Arabs live in wealthy, modern urban centers like Doha, the capital of Qatar, one of the richest nations on earth. If we only see people who are poorer than us as needy, it is implied arrogance. What if the wealthy don't need our water wells? Our pride can keep us away form those who look down upon us; our hubris and insecurity sometimes lead us to work among those for whom we can provide. Everybody likes to be a savior. The challenge of the wealthy, urban, unreached Muslim in the Arabian Gulf is often two-edged: Not only does Islam bind them, but they also need absolutely nothing practical from us. We are forced to preach the gospel in utter weakness.

To live dead is to journey. It is not momentary heroism or occasional folly; it is a life dedicated to following Jesus—no matter the cost. We are not the first to embark on this journey; we follow in the footsteps of Paul, the Celts, Franciscans, Moravians, Carey, Taylor, Elliot, Townsend, McGavran, Winter, and thousands of colleagues from the Global South. No, we are not the first, but we very well could be the last. If we are joyfully willing to pay any price—to live or die—that Jesus be glorified by every people everywhere, then the end shall come.

LIVE DEAD IN THE ARAB CONTEXT

The Sudanese have a poignant proverb: "If you want to kill an elephant, you cannot stab its shadow." Jesus taught a similar truth when He observed that if you want to plunder the strong man's house, you first have to bind the strong man. The premier challenge to the gospel in our age is Islam. The heart of Islam is the Arab world. The financial center (petrol dollars), the emotional center (Mecca), and the ideological center (Cairo) all are found in the Arab world. Yes, there are countries with more Muslims in them than Saudi Arabia or Egypt, but if there was a massive revival among Saudi Arabians, it would have more impact on the world of Islam (and beyond) than a similar revival in any other Muslim country.

If we truly want to see the gospel preached in all the world, among every people, we must make a concentrated effort to preach among Muslims. And again, the Muslim center is the Arab world.

European powers in the eighteenth and nineteenth centuries squabbled over access to the Middle East. Trade routes and resources drove France, England, and Russia to intervene and ultimately to colonize the Arab world. Post-World War II bankruptcy led to independence and euphoria among Arab Muslims. This euphoria was short lived as totalitarian governments, selfish monarchies, or despotic dictators replaced colonial masters.

In 2011, revolutions spread across the Arab world. These successive revolts (which started in Tunisia and spread to Libya, Egypt, Yemen, Syria, and beyond) came to be known as the Arab Spring. Arabs, Muslim and Christian, rose up to throw off oppressive yokes and were both surprised and elated at their success—some revolutions more successful than others. Joy turned to despair and despair to anger, however, as into the vacuum stepped highly organized Islamic movements. These Islamic parties were swept to power through democratic processes and then, ironically, used their mandate to impose Islamic law and with it, coercion. The possibility of freedom and its quick removal was, and is, more painful than the original oppression.

While the unfolding events may be ominous for human rights and basic freedoms, they are incredibly opportunistic for the gospel. Arab Muslims as a whole are disappointed and searching. For the first time, they are daring to think, seek, question, and search for ultimate answers—even outside Islam. Never have we seen so much interest in the gospel, never have we seen so many Arab Muslims turn to Jesus. Now is the time to invest in the Arab world.

Live Dead as a specific missions strategy began in Sudan and was then broadened to include people groups across East Africa. The next Live Dead wave was the Arab world. Many organizations and missions have been active in the Arab world for decades, and Live Dead Arab World is intentional about Kingdom partnership with those already working in the Arab world, and those who will come.

The ultimate goal is to preach the gospel of the Kingdom among every people group on earth that Jesus might come back (Matthew 24:14). We believe the best way to do this is by working toward church planting movements among every ethno-linguistic people. We want to link with others who share the same vision. We dedicate ourselves to God's team and His body as we pursue this common goal. Phase 1 was a church planting training team in Cairo. That was expanded to include training teams in Morocco, Jordan, and Oman. Phase 2 is a church planting teams in thirty-three gateway cities that have over one million people and are centers of commerce, culture, and influence. Phase 3 is a church planting team among every people in the Arab world. Where others are already working, we will seek to join them; where we arrive first, we will open our hearts and homes to others.

The current instability of the Arab world is no deterrent. This is our new reality. The gospel must ever go forth under pressure. It is a joy and a privilege to lift up Jesus in an hour that is so precarious. The long-term safety of our teams is ever on our minds but not primary in our hearts. Our priority is to glorify God, proclaim the gospel boldly and widely, and allow God's character to be formed in us. Only after all of these are attended to do we consider our personal security and safety. As soon as our security becomes our initial priority, we will have missed what it means and costs to live dead, and we will not see the gospel preached in the Arab world, nor among every people, nor will the end come.

Live Dead in the Arab world is a joyful embracing of what will be—and its difficult means—for the joy set before us, for the glory of God among all peoples.

SUGGESTED READING LIST
FOR EXTRAVAGANT DAILY TIMES WITH JESUS

OSWALD CHAMBERS
My Utmost for His Highest
*If You Will Ask: Reflections on the Power of
    Prayer*

FRANCIS CHAN
Crazy Love: Overwhelmed by a Relentless God
Multiply: Disciples Making Disciples
*Forgotten God: Reversing Our Tragic Neglect
    of the Holy Spirit*

GENE EDWARDS
The Divine Romance
A Tale of Three Kings
Living Close to God
Revolution: The Story of the Early Church

JOHN ELDREDGE
*The Utter Relief of Holiness: How God's
    Goodness Frees Us from Everything that
    Plagues Us*
*Beautiful Outlaw: Experiencing the Playful,
    Disruptive, Extravagant Personality of
    Jesus*
Epic: The Story God Is Telling
*Desire: The Journey We Must Take to Find
    the Love God Offers*

FRANÇOIS FÉNELON
The Seeking Heart
The Inner Life
Talking with God

RICHARD FOSTER
*Longing for God: Seven Paths of Christian
    Devotion*
*Celebration of Discipline: The Path to
    Spiritual Growth*
Prayer: Finding the Heart's True Home
*Sanctuary of the Soul: Journey into Meditative
    Prayer*
*Life with God: Reading the Bible for Spiritual
    Transformation*

CHRISTOPHER HEUERTZ
*Unexpected Gifts: Discovering the Way of
    Community*
*Friendship at the Margins: Discovering
    Mutuality in Service and Missions*
*Simple Spirituality: Learning to See God in a
    Broken World*

C. S. LEWIS
*A Year with C. S. Lewis: Daily Readings
    from His Classic Works*
Mere Christianity
Reflections on the Psalms
Miracles

CALVIN MILLER
*Into the Depths of God: Where Eyes See
    the Invisible, Ears Hear the Inaudible,
    and Minds Conceive the Unconceivable*
The Disciplined Life
*Loving God Up Close: Rekindling Your
    Relationship with the Holy Spirit*
*A Hunger for the Holy: Nurturing Intimacy
    with Christ*

WANG MING DAO
A Call to the Church
A Stone Made Smooth

JOHN PIPER
The Pursuit of God
Future Grace
Risk Is Right: Better to Lose Your Life than
*   to Waste It*
Think: The Life of the Mind and the Love
*   of God*
A Hunger for God: Desiring God Through
*   Fasting and Prayer*
Future Grace: The Purifying Power of the
*   Promises of God*
Let the Nations Be Glad: The Supremacy of
*   God in Missions*

CORRIE TEN BOOM
The Hiding Place
Amazing Love: True Stories of the Power of
*   Forgiveness*
I Stand at the Door and Knock: Meditations
*   by Corrie ten Boom*

A. W. TOZER
The Pursuit of God
The Knowledge of the Holy
God's Pursuit of Man
Man, the Dwelling Place of God
The Purpose of Man
Mornings with Tozer: A 366 Day Devotional

Mark Renfroe and his wife, Amy, have served in the Arab world for more than twenty years. They have four wonderful children—Noor, Habeeb, Nabil, and Emad. When asked why they gave them Arabic names, Mark and Amy's answer is simple: "When God called us to the Arab world, He gave us heart transplants. He gave us the heart of an Arab man and woman. After all, you can't really reach people you don't love." Mark surrendered to the grace of God at the age of twenty-two, and the one thing that keeps him going is the indescribable love of God that was ultimately demonstrated through the cross.

Dick Brogden and his wife, Jennifer, have been treasuring Jesus among Muslims in Mauritania (1992), Kenya (1993-95), Sudan (1995-2011), and North Africa (since 2011). Their two sons, Luke and Zack, were born in Sudan and consider themselves Africans. The Brogdens love Jesus with all their broken hearts and long that every ancient gate may be lifted up that Jesus, strong and mighty, King of Glory, may come in. They believe that God is best glorified in mission when His people work in multinational teams to reach the unreached and to plant the church where Christ has not been named.

Jackie A. Chapman has discovered that a gift for words and storytelling is valuable to church planting among Muslims of the Arab world, and she finds great joy in helping young people connect the dots between their gifts and passions and reaching the unreached. Prior to serving in the Arab world, Jackie worked for fourteen years as a magazine editor and music journalist in Nashville, Tenn.

Special thanks to...

Omar Beiler for leadership to the Eurasia Region, our missionaries across the Arab world for their words, Randy Bacon for his superb photography and cinematography efforts for Live Dead, Noor Barron and Shannon Varis for their beautiful photography used throughout this book, Austin Evans, Gabe Tenneson, Josh Tenneson, and Michael Buesking for their artistic contributions to this journey, and Prodgy Pixel's design team who brought the Live Dead stories and artwork to life in these pages.